Author of:

1.) "Correcting Distortions of The Bible" by Kathryn Jordyn

2.) "The Purpose of The Fall" by Kathryn Jordyn

3.) "The Law of One- Condensed: Book 1" by Kathryn Jordyn

4.) "The Law of One- Condensed: Book 2" by Kathryn Jordyn

5.) "The Law of One- Condensed: Book 3" by Kathryn Jordyn

6.) "The Law of One- Condensed: Book 4" by Kathryn Jordyn

7.) "The Law of One- Condensed: Book 5" by Kathryn Jordyn

8.) All 5 Law of One books combined, plus 150 pages of bonus channelings from the Galactic Federation found in the book called: Extraterrestrial Wisdom- by Jorden *. All 5 condensed Law of One books individually would cost $50, this combined book is $37. The original version is $80 without the definitions included. Extraterrestrial Wisdom is a book of Channeled Messages to help Humanity.

Law of One- Condensed

Book 3

(Easier to Read & Understand Version.)

By Kathryn Jordyn

~FOREWORD~

On January 15, 1981, the channeling group of Don, Carla and Jim started receiving a communication from the social memory complex Ra. From this communication precipitated *The Law of One* and some of the distortions of *The Law of One.*

The pages of this book contain communications received in Sessions 51 through 75 and then translated to an easier to understand condensed version by Kathryn Jordyn in order for the world to understand this significant material easier, as this information is the key to our evolution, healing and a more enlightened society.

This material presupposes a point of view that L/L research has developed in the course of many years of study of the UFO phenomenon. There are 50 previous sessions with Ra that are in books 1 and 2 of this 5-book series. If at all possible, it is good to begin with the beginning of books 1 and 2 before beginning this material, since concepts build upon previous concepts. The Ra contact continued for 106 sessions, which were printed into four books in The Law of One series. Book 5 is the material the group originally omitted from the four books. Now Jordyn has condensed this material and translated it into an easier to understand version as well, since Ra appeared to speak in a PhD level of understanding and understanding beyond what humans have previously heard or understood; an intellect beyond this world.

Book 3 of The Law of One is an intensive study of the techniques of balancing of the energy centers and efficient polarization as our planet makes ready for harvest into fourth density. The nature of time/space and space/time is examined, and some of the ramifications of meditation and magic are discussed. A good deal of material about psychic attack and the Orion group is included, and the volume ends with a beginning glance into the archetypical mind.

L/L Research (The Channeling group) of Don Elkins (The Questioner) Jim McCarty (The Scribe) and Carla L. Rueckert (McCarty) The Channeler first received this information from Ra in 1981. This group are all 5th/6th density Wanderers. These Wanderers are beings from higher densities that came to our 3rd density Earth through reincarnation as an infant in order to one day spread this information for the betterment of humanity.

The magical personality (a being of unity, 6th density, equivalent to Higher Self and a personality enormously rich in variety of experiences and subtlety of emotion.)

Session 51: 5-13-1981

Ra: "I am Ra. In time of harvest there are always harvesters. The fruit is formed as it will be, but there is some supervision necessary to ensure that this bounty is placed as it should be without the bruise or the blemish."

There are those of three levels watching over harvest.

The first level is planetary and that which may be called angelic. This type of guardian includes the mind/body/spirit complex totality or Higher Self of an entity and those inner plane entities which have been attracted to this entity through its inner seeking.

The second class of those who ward this process are those of the Confederation who have the honor/duty of standing in the small places at the edge of the steps of light/love so that those entities being harvested will not, no matter how confused or unable to make contact with their Higher Self, stumble and fall away for any reason other than the strength of the light. These Confederation entities catch those who stumble and set them aright so that they may continue into the light.

The third group watching over this process are the Guardians. This group is from the octave above our own and serves in this manner as light bringers. These Guardians provide the precise emissions of light/love in exquisitely fastidious (accurate) disseminations (spreading) of discrimination so that the precise light/love vibration of each entity may be ascertained (determined).

Thus, the harvest is automatic in that those harvested will respond according to that which is unchangeable during harvest. That is the violet-ray emanation. However, these helpers are around to ensure a proper harvesting so that each entity may have the fullest opportunity to express its violet-ray selfhood."

Ra: "Those for the most part coming from other planets do not need craft as you know them. Firstly, there are a few third-density entities who have learned how to use craft to travel between star systems while experiencing the limitations you now understand. However, such entities have learned to use hydrogen in a way different from your understanding now. These entities still take quite long durations of time to move about. However, these entities are able to use hypothermia to slow the physical and mental complex processes in order to withstand the duration of flight. Those such as are from Sirius of this type. There are two other types.

One is the type which, coming from fourth, fifth, or sixth density in your own galaxy, has access to a type of energy system which uses the speed of light as a slingshot and thus arrives where it wishes without any perceptible time elapsed in your view.

The other type of experience is that of fourth, fifth, and sixth densities of other galaxies and some within your own galaxy which have learned the necessary disciplines of personality to view the universe as one being and, therefore, are able to proceed from locus (location) to locus (location) by thought alone, materializing the necessary craft to enclose the light body of the entity."

The Orion group is mixed between the penultimate (next-to-last) and the latter groups.

Humans have seven bodies each corresponding to one of the seven colors of the spectrum. The energy that creates these seven bodies is a universal type of energy that streams into our planetary environment and comes in through the seven energy centers called chakras to develop and perfect these bodies. Each of these bodies is related to our mental configuration (between spirit and mind or body and mind upon many different levels) and through this mental configuration we may block, to some extent, the instreamings of energy that created these seven bodies.

Each energy center has seven sub-colors for convenience. Thus, spiritual/mental blockages combined with mental/bodily blockages may affect each of the energy centers in several different ways. Thus, you may see the subtle nature of the balancing and evolutionary process.

On the back of the book Secrets of the Great Pyramid, there are several reproductions of Egyptian drawings or works, some showing birds flying over horizontal entities. Ra said these drawings are some of many that distort the teaching of our perception of death as the gateway to further experience.

The distortion of Gnosticism is the belief that one may achieve knowledge and a proper position by means of a carefully perceived and accentuated (highlighted) movements, concepts and symbols. In fact, the process of the physical death is where there is aid available, and the only need at death is the releasing of that entity from its body by those around it and the praising of the process by those who grieve. By this may the mind/body/spirit that experienced physical death be aided, not by the various perceptions of careful and repeated rituals.

In the first three energy centers a full unblocking of energy centers will create speeds of rotation. As the entity develops the higher energy centers, these centers will then begin to express their nature by forming crystal structures. This is the higher or more balanced form of activation of energy centers as this space/time energy is transmuted to regularization and balance in time/space.

(Our true nature appears to be crystallized energy centers in space/time but in time/space they only need to be balanced and not perfect.)

Each of the energy centers of the physical complex may be seen to have a distinctive crystalline structure in the more developed entity.

Red ray- Spoked wheel energy center.

Orange ray- Orange 3-petal flower.

Yellow ray- Many faceted rounded-star.

Green ray- lotus shape. Number of points of crystalline structure dependent on the strength of this center.

Blue ray- Capable of having perhaps one-hundred facets and great flashing brilliance.

Indigo ray- A quieter center. Basic triangular or 3-petaled shape in many, although some adepts who have balanced the lower energies may create more faceted forms.

Violet ray- The least variable and sometimes described as thousand petaled, as it is the sum of the mind/body/spirit complex.

Each of the energy centers of the physical complex may be seen to have a distinctive crystalline structure in the more developed entity.

Immediately after the physical death the primary activated body is the indigo, the form-maker. The indigo body is the analog for intelligent energy. It is, in microcosm, the Logos. The intelligent energy of the mind/body/spirit complex totality draws its existence from intelligent infinity or the Creator. This Creator is understood both in macrocosm (universe) and microcosm (individual person) to have two natures: the unpotentiated infinity which is intelligent; this is all that there is. (Microcosm is a community, place, or situation regarded as encapsulating in miniature the characteristic qualities or features of something much larger, such as the universe, which is the macrocosm.)

Free will has potentiated as co-Creators with intelligent infinity that has will. The indigo body (form-making body) may use its wisdom to choose the appropriate locus and type of experience which the co-Creator or sub-sub-Logos (person) will take.

Session 52: 5-19-1981

Ra: "The other type of experience is the fourth, fifth, and sixth densities of other solar systems, and some within our own Solar System has learned necessary disciplines of personality to view the universe as one being are able to proceed from locus (location) to locus (location) by thought alone, materializing the necessary craft."

Other solar systems are not more capable of manipulating the dimensions than our own solar System. It is merely that there are other systems besides our own.

The terminology of right and left brain has inaccuracies. Some functions are repetitive in both lobes and to some entities the functions are reversed.

Ra: "The technology of which you, as a social complex, are so enamored (infatuated) at this time is but the birthing of the manipulation of the intelligent energy of the sub-Logos which, when carried much further, may evolve into technology capable of using the gravitic effects of which we spoke.

We note that this term is not accurate, but there is no closer term. Therefore, the use of technology to manipulate outside the self is far, far less of an aid to personal evolution than the disciplines of the mind/body/spirit complex resulting in the whole knowledge of the self in the microcosm (self) and macrocosm (whole universe).

To the disciplined entity, all things are open and free. The discipline which opens the universes opens also the gateways to evolution. The difference is that of choosing either to hitchhike to a place where beauty may be seen, or to walk, step by step, independent and free in this independence to praise the strength to walk and the opportunity for the awareness of beauty.

The hitchhiker, instead, is distracted by conversation and the vagaries (unexpected changes) of the road and, dependent upon the whims of others, is concerned to make the appointment in time. The hitchhiker sees the same beauty but has not prepared itself for the establishment, in the roots of mind, of the experience."

The positively oriented 4th and 5th density social memory complexes will be attempting to learn disciplines of mind, body, and spirit to accomplish travel. However, there are some technologies available to use intelligent energy forces to accomplish travel, do so while learning the more appropriate disciplines.

A much higher percentage of positively oriented social memory complexes use the personality disciplines, such as thought, to accomplish travel.

Fifth density that moves into sixth has virtually no entities that use outer technology for travel or communication.

The fourth-density negative uses the slingshot gravitic light effect, perhaps 80 percent of its membership being unable to master the disciplines necessary for alternate methods of travel.

In fifth-density negative, approximately 50% at some point gain the necessary discipline to use thought to accomplish travel.

As the sixth density approaches, the negative orientation is thrown into confusion and little travel is attempted. What travel is done is perhaps 73% light/thought.

There are patent differences between positive and negative densities close to the end of fifth density in the disciplines in personality in the completion of the knowledge of the self, necessary to accomplish this discipline.

Discipline of the personality is the acceptance of self; forgiveness of self and the direction of the will is the path towards the disciplined personality. Your faculty of will is that which is powerful within you as a co-Creator, it must be carefully used and directed in service to others for those on the positive path.

There is great danger in the use of will as the personality becomes stronger, for it may be used even subconsciously in ways reducing the polarity of the entity.

Discipline of the personality (acceptance of self, forgiveness of self, and the direction of the will) has the knowledge of self and strengthening of the will is important in third through early seventh densities.

It is paramount to know that it is not desirable or helpful to the growth of the understanding of an entity by itself to control thought processes or impulses except where they may result in actions not consonant with the Law of One. Control may seem to be a shortcut to discipline, peace, and illumination. However, this very control potentiates and necessitates the further incarnative experience in order to balance this control or repression of the self which is perfect.

There is a chance for an entity to remember what was lost in the forgetting by reincarnating again, there is a nimiety (surplus) of opportunity for positive polarization.

Ra: "I am Ra. There are several reasons for incarnation during harvest. They may be divided by the term's "self" and "other self."

The overriding reason for the offering of these Brothers and Sisters of Sorrow in incarnative states is the possibility of aiding other selves by the lightening of the planetary consciousness distortions and the probability of offering catalyst to other selves which will increase the harvest. (This means that the reason the Brothers and Sisters of Sorrow of higher density positive beings that hear people's prayers or cries for help might incarnate into Earth as babies is for the possibility of helping people on Earth raise their positive polarity to increase graduation here on Earth at the Harvest.)

There are two other reasons for choosing this service which have to do with the self.

The Wanderer, if it remembers and dedicates itself to service, will polarize much more rapidly than is possible in the far more etiolated (pale and drawn out due to lack of light) realms of higher-density catalyst.

The final reason is within the mind/body/spirit totality or the social memory complex totality which may judge that an entity or members of a societal entity can make use of third-density catalyst to recapitulate (summarize and retell) a learning/teaching which is adjudged (determined) to be less than perfect. This especially applies to those entering into and proceeding through sixth density, wherein the balance between compassion and wisdom is perfected."

The slingshot effect is energy put into the craft until it approaches the velocity of light, which requires more and more energy. Time dilation occurs by moving 90 degrees to the direction of travel it's possible to change this stored energy in its application of direction to move out of space/time (physical) into time/space (invisible/metaphysical) with a 90-degree deflection. Then, the energy would be taken out in time/space (metaphysical or another dimension) and you would reenter space/time (physical in our dimension) at the end of this energy burst. Due to the questioner's training, Ra stated that he (Don) is more able than Ra to express this concept that the questioner Don thought of. Ra added that the 90 degree is an angle that may be best understood as a portion of a tesseract.

Ra said that we are all one. This is the great learning/teaching. In this unity lies love. This is a great learn/teaching. In this unity lies light. This is the fundamental teaching of all planes of existence in materialization. Unity, love, light, and joy; this is the heart of evolution of the spirit.

The second-ranking lessons are learned/taught in meditation and in service. At some point the mind/body/spirit complex is so smoothly activated and balanced by these central thoughts of unity love, light and joy that disciplines of personality and knowledge of self, universe, its mystery unbroken, is one. Always begin and end in the Creator not technique such as the disciplines of personality, which is acceptance of self, forgiveness of self, strengthening of will and knowledge of self.

There are light bringers from the octave above ours. They provide the light for the graduation of an octave into 8th density, which is the 1st density into a new octave. This octave density above ours is both omega and alpha, the spiritual mass of the infinite universes becoming one central sun or Creator once again. This births a new universe, a new infinity, a new Logos which incorporates all that the Creator has experienced of Itself. There are also Wanderers in this new octave. Ra knowns very little across the boundary of octave except that these beings come to aid our octave in its Logos completion.

Session 53: 5-25-1981

Ra stated that at the current limit of the instrument's strength, physical exercise is well in the long run due to cumulative building up of vital energies. The short run is wearying to the entity (until the buildup occurs).

The physical difficulties (of Carla) prior to contact with Ra are due to the action of the subconscious will of the instrument. This will is extremely strong and requires the mind/body/spirit complex to reserve all available physical and vital energies for the contact. Thus, the discomforts are experienced due to the dramatic distortion towards physical weakness while this energy is diverted. The entity is also under psychic attack, and this intensifies preexisting conditions and is responsible for the cramping and the dizziness as well as mind complex distortions.

Before someone attends a session, they may have special meditative periods set aside before an entity sits within a working. Ra suggests a photograph of all members in the group be sent to the entity wanting to join with writing indicating love and light upon it. This held while meditating will bring the entity into peaceful harmony with each of the group members so that there be no extraneous waste of energy while greetings are exchanged between two entities, both of whom have a distortion towards solitude and shyness.

The most efficient mode of contact from positively oriented Confederation with the people of this planet is channeling, such as what was done to obtain this information in this book from Ra. The infringement upon free will is greatly undesired. Therefore, Wanderers upon our plane of illusion will be the only ones for thought projections that make up the so-called social memory complexes and Wanderers.

An example of a meeting between a social memory complex and a Wanderer is that of the one known as Morris (Case #1 in Secrets of the UFO, 1976, pp 10-11). Morris' circle of friends experienced a negatively oriented contact. However, Morris was impervious to this contact and could not see, with the physical optical apparatus, this contact.

However, the inner voice alerted Morris to go by itself to another place, and there an entity with a thought form shape and appearance of the other contact appeared and gazed at Morris, thus awakening in it the desire to seek the truth of this occurrence and of the experiences of its incarnation in general.

Landed thought form Confederation UFO crafts have occurred but is much less common than the Orion type of so-called Close Encounter. Ra states that in a universe of unending unity, the concept of a "Close Encounter" is humorous because all encounters of self is with the self (others.) "Therefore, how can any encounter be less than very very close?" Ra asks.

The feeling of being awakened or activated is the goal of this type of positive contact. The duration and imagery used varies depending upon the subconscious expectations of the Wanderer which is experiencing this opportunity for activation.

Talking of encounters of self with self, positively oriented Wanderers have had a Close Encounter with the Orion or negatively oriented polarization. When it occurs, it is quite rare and occurs either due to Orion entities lack of perception of the depth of positivity to be encountered or due to their desire to attempt to remove this positivity from this plane of existence. Orion tactics normally choose the simple distortions of mind which indicate less mental and spiritual complex activity.

The methods used to awaken Wanderers are varied. The center of each approach is the entrance into the conscious and subconscious in a way to avoid causing fear and to maximize the potential for an understandable subjective experience that has meaning for the entity. Many occur in sleep; others in the midst of many activities during waking hours. The approach is flexible and does not necessarily include the "Close Encounter" syndrome as people are aware of.

The subconscious expectations of entities cause the nature and detail of thought form experience offered by Confederation thought form entities. If a Wanderer expects a physical examination, it will perforce (unescapably) be experienced with as little distortion towards alarm or discomfort as is allowable by the expectation of the subconscious distortions of the Wanderer.

The Orion group uses the physical examination as a means of terrifying the individual and causing it to feel feelings of advanced second-density being such as a laboratory animal. The sexual experiences of some are a subtype of this experience. Their intent is to demonstrate the control of the Orion entities over the Terran inhabitant.

The thought form experiences are subjective and, for the most part, do not occur in third density.

There is a large spectrum of entities on Earth that are harvestable both negatively and positively.

Ra: "The most typical approach of Orion entities is to choose the weaker-minded entity that it might suggest a greater amount of Orion philosophy to be disseminated.

Some few Orion entities are called by more highly polarized negative entities of your space/time nexus. In this case they share information just as we are now doing. However, this is a risk for the Orion entities due to the frequency with which the harvestable negative planetary entities then attempt to bid and order the Orion contact just as these entities bid planetary negative contacts. The resulting struggle for mastery, if lost, is damaging to the polarity of the Orion group.

Similarly, a mistaken Orion contact with highly polarized positive entities can wreak havoc with Orion troops unless these

19

Crusaders are able to depolarize the entity mistakenly contacted. This occurrence is almost unheard of. Therefore, the Orion group prefers to make physical contact only with the weaker-minded entity."

If there is fear and doom "Close Encounter," the contact was quite likely negative. If the result is hope, friendly feelings, and the awakening of a positive feeling of purposeful service to others, marks of Confederation contact are evident.

Fourth-density Confederation entity looks variously (differently) depending on the derivation (origin) of its physical vehicle.

Confederation entities that can pass as humans most often are fifth-density positive. Fifth-density negative Orion's can pass as humans as well if they choose to take on a similar human form.

Session 54: 5-29-1981

From the Logos comes all frequencies of radiation of light. These frequencies of radiation make up all the densities of experience that are created by that Logos.

The total experience created by our Sun is the planetary system (or solar system) in all of its densities.

The different frequencies are separated into the seven colors. Each of these colors is the basic frequency for a sub-sub-Logos (an individual) to activate on of these basic frequencies or colors and use that body that is generated from the activation of the frequency or color.

Sub-Sub Logos resides only in co-Creators (mind/body/spirit complexes) not in dimensionalities (dimensions). A person can have any body activated of the seven rays, each true color vehicle is available, potentially there is skill and discipline needed in order to avail the self of the more

20

advanced or lighter vehicles. Just like skill is needed to be able to offer concerts.

There's intelligent energy coming from the sub-Logos (the Sun). This intelligent energy is somehow modulated (fine-tuned) or distorted so that it ends up a mind/body/spirit complex with certain distortions that are necessary for the mental portion of that complex to undistort in order to conform once more with the original intelligent energy.

In the free will of self (you) knowing self (another person) you may begin to distinguish the hallmark of an Infinite Creator. If there were no potentials for misunderstanding or understanding, there would be no experience.

Once an entity becomes aware of this process, it then decides that in order to have the full abilities of the Creator it is necessary to have a balanced blending of energy centers with the Original Creative Thought in precise vibration. The precision of each energy center matching the Original Thought lies in the balanced blending of these energy centers in such a way that intelligent energy is able to channel itself with minimal distortion. The mind/body/sprit complex is not a machine. It is rather a tone poem.

All mind/body/spirit complexes in the Infinite Creation has seven energy centers in potential in macrocosm from the beginning of creation by the Logos. Coming out of timelessness, all is prepared. This is so of the Infinite Creation.

The Logos creates light. This light creates the catalytic and energetic levels of experiences in the creation. The highest of all honor/duties (given in the next octave) is the supervision of light in its manifestations during experimental times of our cycles. (Known as the 8th density)

The Mind/body/spirit complex may choose the mental configuration sufficiently displaced from the configuration of the intelligent energy in a particular frequency or color of instreaming energy so as to block a portion of instreaming energy that blocks the frequency or color.

In an entity's pattern of instreaming energy, there may be a complete blockage in an energy center or color or combination of energies or colors.

Free will is the motivator for this energy blockage. Ra prefers to avoid the word "to allow". Free will does not allow, nor would predetermination disallow experiential distortions from blockages. Rather, the Law of Confusion/Free Will offers a free reach of each entity. The verb "to allow" would be considered pejorative (limitation) in that it suggests a polarity between right and wrong or allowed and not allowed. (There is no right or wrong. We are not restricted from anything.) This may seem a minuscule point. However, to Ra's best way of thinking it bears weight Ra says.

It is primary priority to activate or unblock each energy center and begin to refine the balances between the energies so that each tone of the chord of total vibrating beingness resonates in clarity, tune, and harmony with each other energy. This balancing, tuning and harmonizing of the self is most central to the more advanced or advanced mind/body/spirit complex. Each energy center may be activated without the disciplines and appreciations of the deeper personality or soul identity.

Analogy: A seven-stringed musical instrument may be played by deflecting each string and releasing it, producing notes. The individual creative personality could deflect each string the proper amount in the proper sequence, producing music.

In the balanced individual the energies lie waiting for the hand of the Creator to pluck harmony.

The sub-Logos offers the catalyst at the lower levels of energy. The first triad has to do with the survival of the physical complex. The higher centers gain catalyst from the biases of the mind/body/spirit complex itself in response to all random and directed experiences.

Thus, the less developed entity will perceive the catalyst about it in terms of survival of the physical complex with the preferred distortions. The more conscious entity of the catalytic process will begin to transform the catalyst offered by the sub-Logos into catalyst that may act upon the higher-energy nexi. So, the sub-Logos can offer only a basic skeleton of catalyst. The muscles and flesh having to do with the survival of wisdom, love, compassion and service are brought about by the action of the individual on basic complex so as to create a more complex catalyst which may form distortions within these higher energy centers.

The more advanced the entity, the more tenuous (thin/weaker) the connection between the sub-Logos and the perceived catalyst. Until finally, all catalyst is chosen, generated, and manufactured by the self, for the self.

The number of those who have mastered outer catalyst and can manufacture all their catalyst is quite small.

Most of those harvestable at this space/time nexus have partial control over the outer illusion and are using the outer catalyst to work upon some bias which is not yet in balance.

The negatively oriented entity will program catalyst for maximal separation from and control over all those things and conscious entities which it perceives as being other than self. They will ordinarily program for wealth, ease of existence, and the utmost opportunity for power. Thus, many entities burst with health.

However, a negatively oriented entity may choose a painful condition in order to improve the distortions toward the negative emotive mentation's such as anger, hatred, and frustration. Such an entity may use an entire incarnative experience honing a blunt edge of hatred or anger so that it may polarize more towards the negative or separate pole.

A positively oriented entity may select a certain narrow path of thinking and activities during an incarnation and program conditions that would create physical pain if this were not followed.

Prior to incarnation, as an entity becomes more aware of the process of evolution and has selected the positive or negative path, at some point the entity becomes aware of what it wants to unblock and balance its energy centers. It is then able to program for the life experience of those catalytic experiences that will aid it in its process of unblocking and balancing.

The purpose of incarnative existence is evolution of mind, body and spirit. In order to do this, it is not strictly necessary to have catalyst. However, without catalyst the desire to evolve and the faith in the process do not normally manifest, and thus evolution occurs not. Therefore, catalyst is programmed and designed for the mind, body, spirit complex unique requirements. Thus, it is desirable that the entity be aware of the voice of its experiential catalyst, gleaning from it what it incarnated to glean.

The mind, body, spirit complex is the vehicle for experience; and has energy centers needed to keep it in correct conformation and composition. Both negative and positive entities do well to reserve this small portion of each center for the maintenance of the integrity of the mind/body/spirit complex. After this point, the negative will use the three lower centers for separation from and control over others by sexual means, by personal assertion (exercising authority confidently and forcefully) and by action in our societies.

Contrary-wise, the positively oriented entity will be transmuting strong red-ray sexual energy into green-ray energy transfers and radiation in blue and indigo and will be similarly transmuting selfhood and place in society into energy transfer situations in which the entity may merge with and serve others and then, finally, radiate unto others without expecting any transfer in return.

The energy that enters through these energy centers: The origin of all energy is the action of free will upon love. The nature of all energy is light. The means of it is ingress (entering) into the mind/body/spirit complex is duple (paired together).

Firstly, there is the inner light which is Polaris (brightest) of the self, the guiding star. This is the birthright and true nature of all entities. This energy dwells within.

The second point of ingress (entrance) is the polar opposite of the North Star and may be seen, if you wish to use the physical body as an analog (comparable) for the magnetic field, as coming through the feet from the Earth and through the lower point of the spine. This point of ingress (entrance) of the universal light energy is undifferentiated (not different) until it begins its filtering process through the energy centers. The requirements of each energy center and the efficiency with which the individual has learned to tap into the inner light determine the nature of the use made by the entity of these instreaming.

The experiential catalyst and the requirements or distortions of the energy centers are two concepts linked as lightly as two strands of rope. The experiential catalyst is first experienced by the south pole and appraised with respect to its survival value. As Ra stated earlier, there's a filtering process by which incoming energies are pulled upwards according to the distortions of each energy center and the strength of will or desire emanating from the awareness of inner fight.

The total energy that the mind/body/spirit complex will receive in the way of light comes through the feet and base of spine. Each energy center then filters out and uses a portion of this energy, red through indigo. The violet ray is a thermometer or indicator of the whole.

In the fully activated entity, only that small portion of instreaming light needed to tune the energy center is used, the great remainder being free to be channeled and attracted upwards.

As this energy is absorbed into the being it radiates upwards beginning with the blue ray, although the green ray, being the great transitional ray, must be given all careful consideration, for until transfer of energy of all types has been experienced and mastered to a great extent, there will be blockages in the blue and indigo radiations.

Again, the violet emanation is a resource from which, through indigo, intelligent infinity may be contacted. The radiation will be green, blue or indigo depending on the type of intelligence infinity has brought through into discernible (perceivable) energy.

The green-ray type is the healing, the blue ray the communication and inspiration, the indigo energy of the adept that has its place in faith.

A mind/body/spirit complex feeling the activating sensation at the indigo center during meditation is experiencing instreaming's at that energy center to be used either for the unblocking of this center, for its tuning to match the harmonics of its other energy centers, or to activate the gateway to intelligent infinity.

Session 54: 6-5-1981

The psychic support of the (channeling) group towards appreciation and caring for all within the channeling group was the greatest aid to the discomfort of psychic attacks (of Carla). Ra stated that the group subconsciously had true attitudinal (mindset/opinion), mental, emotional and spiritual distortions towards the instrument. There is no magic greater than honest distortion toward love.

(The groups love towards Carla, the instrument, helped her discomfort from the psychic attacks from negative entities trying to discourage her from getting this information out.)

The negative polarization is greatly aided by the subjugation (control) or enslavement of other selves. The potential between two negatively polarized entities is one enslaving the other or bids the others then gains in negative polarity.

The entity bidden or enslaved, in serving an other self, will lose negative polarity although it will gain in desire for further negative polarization. This desire will then tend to create opportunities to regain negative polarity.

In the calling of an Orion Crusader, the entity that calls is a suppliant (requester) neophyte (newcomer) asking for aid in negative understanding. The Orion response increases its negative polarity as it is disseminating the negative philosophy, thereby enslaving or bidding the entity that is calling.

In the instance where the contact becomes contest (competition for power), which is prototypical (typical example) of negativity, the call will attempt not to ask for aid, but to demand results. Since the third-density negatively oriented harvestable entity has at its disposal an incarnative experiential nexus and since Orion Crusaders are, in a great extent, bound by the first distortion of free will in order to progress, the Orion entity is vulnerable to such bidding if properly done. In this case, the third-density entity becomes master and the Orion Crusader becomes entrapped and can be bid. This is rare. However, when it has occurred, the Orion entity or social memory complex involved has experienced loss of negative polarity by the strength of the bidding third-density entity.

To properly bid is to be properly negative. The percentage of thought and behavior involving service to self must approach 99 percent in order for a third-density negative entity to be properly configured for such a contest of bidding.

The two most usual types of bidding are the use of perversions of sexual magic and the use of perversions of ritual magic. In each case the key to success is the purity of the will of the bidder. The concentration on victory over the servant must be nearly perfect.

There is no relationship between a channeling contact and the bidding process. The Ra contact may be characterized as the Brothers and Sisters of Sorrow, wherein those receiving the contact have attempted to prepare for such contact by sacrificing extraneous (external), self-oriented distortions in order to be of service.

The Ra social memory complex offers itself also as a function of its desire to serve. Both the caller and the contact are filled with gratitude at the opportunity of serving others. This in no way presupposes (assumes) that either the callers or those of Ra's group in any way approach a perfection or purity such as the bidding process described as 99% negative. The calling group may have many distortions and the working with much catalyst, as may those of Ra. The overriding desire to serve others, bonded with the unique harmonics of this group's vibratory complexes, gives Ra the opportunity to serve as one channel for the One Infinite Creator.

Things come not to those positively oriented but through such beings.

Ra stated that "As we (Ra) had been aided by shapes such as the pyramid, so we could aid your people." Ra stated, "You will find the intersection of the triangle which is at the first level on each of the four sides forms a diamond in a plane which is horizontal."

The purpose of the pyramid shape is to work with time/space portions of the mind/body/spirit complex. Therefore, the intersection is both space/time (physical) and time/space (non-physically) oriented and is expressed in three-dimensional geometry by two intersections, which projected in both time/space (non-physical/metaphysical) and space/time (physical), from one point.

Don Elkins, Carla the questioner calculated this point to be one-sixth of the height of the triangle that forms the side of the pyramid. Ra was pleased at his perspicacity. (Perspicacity is the ability to understand things quickly and make accurate judgments. Someone who is smart.)

The Queen's Chamber in the Great Pyramid at Giza would not be appropriate or useful for healing work, as healing work involves the use of energy in a more synergic (joint) configuration rather than the configuration of the centered being.

Healing work would be done in the King's Chamber.

The chamber below the bottom level of the pyramid below ground, appears to be roughly in line with the King's Chamber. This is a resonating chamber. The bottom of such a structure shall be open, in order to cause the appropriate distortions for healing catalyst.

There is only one significance to the ankh shapes such as the crux ansata; that is, the placing in coded form of mathematical relationships.

The 76 degree and 18' angle at the apex of the pyramid is an appropriate angle for the healing work intended.

Why the King's Chamber have various small chambers above it: The positioning of the entity to be healed is such that the life energies are in a position to be briefly interrupted or intersected by light. By the catalyst of the healer with the crystal,

29

this light then may manipulate the aural forces (the various energy centers) in such a way that if the entity to be healed wills it so, corrections may take place. Then, the entity is re-protected by its own, now less distorted, energy field and is able to go its way.

The process involves bringing the entity to be healed to an equilibrium (a balance). This involves temperature, barometric pressure, and the electrical-charged atmosphere. The first two requirements are controlled by the system of chimneys.

The distorted configuration of the energy centers is intended to be temporarily interrupted, and the opportunity is then presented to the one to be healed to take the balanced route and walk thence with the distortions towards disease of mind, body and spirit greatly lessened.

The catalytic effect of the charged atmosphere and the crystal directed by the healer must be taken into consideration as integral portions of this process, for the bringing back of the entity to a configuration of conscious awareness would not be accomplished after the reorganization possibilities are offered without the healer's presence and directed will.

Session 56: 6-8-1981

Ra: "We are assuming that you wish to know the principle of the shapes, angles, and intersections of the pyramid you call Giza.

In reality, the pyramid shape does no work. It does not work. It is an arrangement for the centralization as well as the diffraction of the spiraling upward light energy as it is being used by the mind/body/spirit complex.

The spiraling nature of light is such that the magnetic fields of an individual are affected by spiraling energy. Certain shapes offer an echo chamber or an intensifier for spiraling prana, as some have called this all-present, primal distortion of the One Infinite Creator.

If the intent is to intensify the necessity for the entity's own will to call forth the inner light in order to match the intensification of the spiraling light energy, the entity will be placed in what you have called the Queen's Chamber position in this particular shaped object. This is the initiatory place and is the place of resurrection.

The offset place, representing the spiral as it is in motion, is the appropriate position for one to be healed, as in this position an entity's vibratory magnetic nexi are interrupted in their normal flux. Thus, a possibility/probability vortex ensues; a new beginning is offered for the entity in which the entity may choose a less distorted, weak, or blocked configuration of energy center magnetic distortion.

The function of the healer and crystal may not be overemphasized, for this power of interruption must need be controlled with incarnate intelligence; the intelligence being that of one which recognizes energy patterns which, without judging, recognizes blockage, weakness, and other distortion and which is capable of visualizing, through the regularity of self and of crystal, the less distorted other self to be healed.

Other shapes which are arched, groined, vaulted, conical (cone-shaped), or, as your tipis, are also shapes with this type of intensification of spiraling light. Your caves, being rounded, are places of power due to this shaping.

Here's a picture of a groined shaped:

Here's a picture of a vaulted ceiling:

It is to be noted that these shapes are dangerous. We are quite pleased to have the opportunity to enlarge upon the subject of shapes such as the pyramid, for we wish, as part of our honor/duty, to state that there are many wrong uses for these curved shapes; for with improper placement, improper intentions, or lack of the crystallized being functioning as channel for healing, the sensitive entity will be distorted more rather than less in some cases.

It is to be noted that your peoples build, for the most part, the cornered or square habitations, for they do not concentrate power. It is further to be noted that the spiritual seeker has, for many of your time periods of years, sought the rounded, arched, and peaked forms as an expression of the power of the Creator."

The most appropriate angle of apex for healing work:

RA: "If the shape is such that it is large enough to contain an individual mind/body/spirit complex at the appropriate offset position within it, the 76 degree 18', approximate, angle is useful and appropriate. If the position varies, the angle may vary. Further, if the healer has the ability to perceive distortions with enough discrimination, the position within any pyramid shape may be moved about until results are affected. However, we found this particular angle to be useful. Other social memory complexes, or portions thereof, have determined different apex angles for different uses, not having to do with healing but with learning. When one works with the cone, or the silo type of shape, the energy for healing may be found to be in a general circular pattern unique to each shape as a function of its particular height and width and in the cone shape, the angle of apex. In these cases, there are no corner angles. Thus, the spiraling energy works in circular motion."

Here's the Silo shape structure:

The spiraling energy is beginning to be diffused at the point where it goes through the King's Chamber in the Giza pyramid. However, although the spirals continue to intersect, closing and opening in double-spiral fashion through the apex angle, the diffusion or strength of the spiraling energies, red through violet color values, lessons in strength and gains of diffusion, until the peak of the pyramid there's a very weak color resolution useful for healing purposes. The King's Chamber position is chosen as the first spiral after the centered beginning through the Queens Chamber position. The diffusion angle is opposite of the pyramid angle, but the angle being less wide than the apex angle of the pyramid, somewhere between 33 degrees and 54 degrees, depending on the various rhythms of the planet itself.

Half of the angle falls on the side of the centerline that the King's Chamber is on, that will indicate (show) the diffusion of the spectrum. The angle will begin somewhere between the Queen's Chamber position and thence (therefrom) downward towards the resonating chamber underground, offset for the healing work.

This variation is dependent upon various magnetic fluxes of the planet. The King's Chamber position is designed to intersect the strongest spiral of the energy flow regardless of where the angle begins. However, as it passes through the Queen's Chamber position, this spiraling energy is always centered and at its strongest point.

Session 57: 6-12-1981

The psychic attack on the instrument (Carla) can potentially be disruptive to this contact for a brief period of our space/time. (This further proves to me that the negative entities causing these attacks do not want this information getting out.)

The instrument had replenished vital energies due to its (her) sense of humor.

The Orion group cannot interfere directly but only through preexisting distortions of mind/body/spirit complexes such as injuries, pain within the body, ect.

The crystal on the ring of the instrument's right hand (her ring) is available (One may use crystals to heal.)

Ra: "You first, as a mind/body/spirit complex, balance and polarize the self, connecting the inner light with the upward spiraling inpourings of the universal light. You have done exercises to regularize the processes involved. Look to them for the preparation of the crystalized being.

Take then the crystal and feel your polarized and potentiated balanced energy channeled in green-ray healing through your being, going into and activating the crystalline regularity of frozen light which is the crystal. The crystal will resound with the charged light of incarnative love, and light energy will begin to radiate in specified fashion, beaming, in required light vibrations, healing energy, focused and intensified towards the magnetic field of the mind/body/spirit complex which is to be healed. This entity requesting such healing will then open the armor of the overall violet/red-ray protective vibratory shield. Thus, the inner vibratory fields, from center to center in mind, body, and spirit, may be interrupted and adjusted momentarily, thus offering the one to be healed the opportunity to choose a less distorted inner complex of energy fields and vibratory relationships."

One may place the crystal (ring) on the necklace so that it hangs around the green-ray energy center; or the chain hung from the right hand, outstretched, wound about the hand in such a way that the crystal may be swung so as to affect sensitive adjustments.

Ra offers this information realizing that much practice is needed to efficiently use these energies of self. However, each has the capability of doing so, and this information is not information which, if followed accurately, can be deleterious (harmful).

The regularized or crystallized entity, in its configuration, is as critical as the perfection of the crystal used.

In some applications concerning planetary healing, the physical size of the crystal has relationship to the effectiveness in the healing. In working with an individual mind/body/spirit complex, the only requirement is that the crystal be in harmony with the crystallized being. There is perhaps a lower limit to the size of a faceted crystal, for light coming through this crystal needs to be spread the complete width of the spectrum of the one to be healed. Water is a type of crystal which is efficacious (effective) also, although not as easy to hang from a chain in our density. (Efficacious is the success of producing a desired or intended result; effective.)

2 to 5.4 centimeters towards the heart is optimal for where the crystal should hang for proper green-ray.

This healing in relation to the healing done in the King's Chamber in the Giza pyramid: Ra says, "There are two advantages to doing this working in such a configuration of shapes and dimensions.

Firstly, the disruption or interruption of the violet/red armoring or protective shell is automatic.

In the second place, the light is configured by the very placement of this position in the seven distinctive color or energy vibratory rates, thus allowing the energy through the crystallized being, focused with the crystal, to manipulate with great ease the undisturbed and carefully delineated (lifelike) palate (bias) of energies or colors, both in space/time and in time/space. Thus, the unarmored (unprotected) being may be adjusted rapidly. This is desirable in some cases, especially when the armoring is the largest moiety (portion) of the possibility of continued function of body complex activity in this density. The trauma of the interruption of this armoring vibration is then seen to be lessened.

We take this opportunity to pursue our honor/duty, as some of those creating the pyramid shape, to note that it is in no way necessary to use this shape in order to achieve healings, for seniority of vibration has caused the vibratory complexes of mind/body/spirit complexes to be healed to be less vulnerable to the trauma of the interrupted armoring (protected shield).

Furthermore, as we have said, the powerful effect of the pyramid, with its mandatory disruption of the armoring, if used without the crystallized being, used with the wrong intention, or in the wrong configuration, can result in further distortions of entities which are perhaps the equal of some of your chemicals which cause disruptions in the energy fields in like manner."

The pyramid may be used for the improvement of the meditative state as long as the shape is in Queen's Chamber position or entities are in balanced configuration about this central point.

The small pyramid shape, placed beneath a portion of the body complex, may energize this body. This should be done for brief periods not to exceed 30 of your minutes.

The use of the pyramid to balance planetary energies still functions to a slight extent, but due to earth changes, the pyramids are no longer aligned properly for this work.

The aid received for meditation by an entity positioned in the Queen's Chamber position: Consider the polarity of mind/body/spirit complexes. The inner light is the heart. Its strength equals your strength of will to seek the light. The position or balanced position of a group intensifies the amount of this will, the amount of awareness of the inner light necessary to attract the instreaming fight upward spiraling from the south magnetic pole of being.

Thus, this is the place of the initiate, for many extraneous items or distortions will leave the entity as it intensifies its seeking,

37

so that it may become one with this centralized and purified incoming light.

A pyramid shape may be smaller if the apex angle is less, thus not allowing the formation of the King's Chamber position. Also efficacious (effective) for this application are the silo, the cone, the dome, and the tipi; these shapes having the Queen's Chamber effect. A strongly crystallized entity is, in effect, a portable King's Chamber position.

If those who desired to be healers were of a crystallized nature and were all supplicants (requester), those wishing less distortion, the pyramid would be, as always, a carefully designed set of parameters to distribute light and its energy so as to aid in healing catalyst.

However, Ra found our peoples are not distorted towards the desire for purity to a great enough extent to be given this powerful and potentially dangerous gift. Ra, therefore, would suggest it not be used for healing in the traditional King's Chamber configuration which Ra stated they naively gave to our peoples only to see it grossly distorted and their teachings lost.

The appropriate apex angle for a tipi shape for our uses: This is at our discretion. The principle of circular, rounded, or peaked shapes is that the center acts as an invisible inductive coil. Thus, the energy patterns are spiraling and circular. Thus, the choice of the most pleasant configuration is ours. The effect is relatively fixed.

The geometry or relationships of these shapes in their configuration is the great consideration. It is well to avoid stannous (containing tin) material or that of lead or other metals. Wood, plastic, glass, and other materials may all be considered to be appropriate.

If the shape of the pyramid is of appropriate size, it may be placed directly under the cushion of the head or the pallet (pillow) that the body rests on.

Ra again cautions that the third spiral of upward-lining light emitted from the apex of this shape, is most deleterious (damaging/harmful) to an entity in overdose and should not be used overlong. (No longer than 30 minutes).

It doesn't matter what the height, in centimeters, of one of the pyramids for best functioning. Only the proportion of the height from the base to the apex to the perimeter of the base is important. The proportion should be the 1.16 which we may observe. Therefore, the sum of the four base sides should be 1.16 of the height of the pyramid.

The queen's Chamber was the initiatory place: Ra cannot describe initiation in its specific sense due to their distortion towards the belief/understanding that the process they offered so many years ago (I would guess 11,000 years ago in Egypt) and was not a balanced one.

However, initiation demands the centering of the being upon the seeking of the Creator. Ra has hoped to balance this understanding by enunciating (articulate) The Law of One; that is, that all things are One Creator. Thus, seeking the Creator is done not just in meditation and in work of an adept but in the experiential nexus of each moment.

The initiation of the Queen's Chamber has to do with the abandoning of self to such desire to know the Creator in full that the purified instreaming light is drawn in balanced fashion through all energy centers, meeting in indigo and opening the gate to intelligent infinity. Thus, the entity experiences true life or resurrection.

The pyramid used for learning is a different process: The difference is the presence of other selves manifesting in space/time and after some study, in time/space, for the purpose of teach/learning. In the system created by Ra, schools were apart from the pyramid, the experiences being solitary.

In Ra's system, experiences in the Queen's Chamber position were solitary. In Atlantis and in South America, teachers shared the pyramid experiences.

There was learning and teaching within the pyramid.

The dangerous pyramid shape for today would be a four-sided pyramid large enough to create the King's Chamber effect. The 76-degree apex angle is that characteristic of the powerful shape.

Any angle less than 70 degrees would not produce this dangerous effect.

Ra: "This instrument has some vital energy left. However, we become concerned with the increasing distortions of the body complex towards pain.

The space/time (physical) and time/space (non-physical/metaphysical) concepts are those concepts mathematically the relationships of your illusion, that which is seen to that which is unseen. These descriptive terms are clumsy. They, however, suffice (are enough) for this work.

In the experiences of the mystical search for unity, these need never be considered, for they are but part of an illusory system. The seeker seeks the One. The One is to be sought, as we have said, by the balanced and self-accepting self-aware, both of its apparent distortions and its total perfection. Resting in this balanced awareness, the entity then opens the self to the universe which it is. The light energy of all things may then be attracted by this intense seeking, and wherever the inner seeking meets the attracted cosmic prana (universal energy which flows vibrationally around the body), realization of the One takes place.

The purpose of clearing each energy center is to allow that meeting place to occur at the indigo-ray vibration, thus making contact with intelligent infinity and dissolving all illusions. Service-to-others is automatic at the released energy generated by this state of consciousness.

The space/time and time/space distinctions do not hold sway except in third density. However, fourth, fifth, and, to some extent, sixth work within some system of polarized space/time and time/space.

The calculation necessary to move from one system to another through the dimensions are somewhat difficult. Therefore, Ra has the most difficulty sharing numerical concepts with us."

Session 58: 6-16-1981

The physical distortion of arthritis in the instrument increased due to over-activity of weak portions of the body.

It is appropriate to use the diamond crystal for healing if the entity is practiced at their healing art. To work with a powerful crystal while unable to perceive the magnetic flux of the subtle bodies, is perhaps the same as recommending that the beginner, with saw and nail, create the Vatican. The crystal healing practices are as previously mentioned: the crystal around the neck near the green ray and dangling the crystal from a chain in the right hand.

There is great art in the use of the swung crystal. A beginner would do well to work with the unpowerful crystals in ascertaining (finding out) not only the physical major energy centers, but also the physical secondary and tertiary energy centers and then begin to find the corresponding subtle body energy centers. In this way, you may activate your own inner vision.

Any dangling weight crystal of symmetrical form can be used by the beginner. Their purpose is not to disturb or manipulate these energy centers but merely to locate them and become aware of what they feel like when in a balanced state and when in an unbalanced state or blocked state.

The distance from hand dangling over body is unimportant and at your discretion. The weight is unimportant as well. The circular motion moving in a clockwise rotational direction shows an unblocked energy center. However, some entities are polarized the reverse of others, and, therefore, it is well to test the form of normal energy spirals before beginning the procedure.

The test is done by first holding the weight over your own hand and observing your particular configuration. Then, using the other self's hand, repeat the procedure. Ra gave general healing information, since there is a line beyond which information is an intrusion upon the Law of Confusion/Free Will.

The pyramid can be in any orientation and provide some focusing of spiraling energy, but the greatest focusing of it occurs when one side of it is precisely parallel to magnetic north. If one corner is oriented to the magnetic north, the energy will be enhanced in its focus also.

The reversed shape of the pyramid reverses the effects of the pyramid. It would only work if an entity's polarity were, for some reason, reversed.

The pyramid shape is a collector which draws the instreaming energy from the base, and allows this energy to spiral upward in a line with the apex of this shape. This is also true if the pyramid shape is upended (flipped over). The energy is not Earth energy, but is light energy, which is omnipresent (present everywhere).

The pyramid, as an energy collector, the shape itself is the only requirement. For the practical needs of our body inside a pyramid, it is well that this shape be solid sided in order to avoid being inundated (flooded) by outer stimuli.

42

The concept of four pieces of wire joined at the apex running down to the base being totally open is equal to the solid form still drawing light energy from the base spiraling upward in a line with the apex of this shape. However, there are many metals not recommended for use in pyramids designed to aid the meditative process. Those recommended is wood, other natural materials, or the man-made plastic rods will also be of service.

A seemingly simple open pyramid with four wooden rods joined at an apex focuses the spiraling light because of the funnel shape.

The third distortion is light. The pyramid shape acts as a funnel increasing the density of energy so that the individual may have a greater intensity of light.

The pure crystalline shape, such as the diamond is frozen light. This third-density physical manifestation of light is somehow a focusing mechanism for the third distortion (light) in a general sense.

However, only the will of the crystallized entity may cause interdimensional light to flow through this material. The more regularized the entity and the crystal, the more profound the effect.

There are many people now bending metal and doing other things like that by mentally requesting this to happen.

This is the influence of the second spiral of light in a pyramid being used by an entity. As this second spiral ends at the apex, the light may be likened unto a laser beam in the metaphysical sense and when intelligently directed may cause bending not only in pyramid, but this is the type of energy tapped into by those capable of this focusing of the upward-spiraling light. This is made possible through contact in indigo ray with intelligent energy.

They have no training and are able to do this. They remember the disciplines necessary for this activity, which is merely useful upon other true color vibratory experiential nexi. The end of such energy focusing is to build, not to destroy, and it does become quite useful as an alternative to third-density building methods.

There are three spirals of light energy which the pyramid exemplifies:

1.) The fundamental spiral- which is used for study and for healing.
2.) The spiral to the apex- used for building.
3.) The spiral spreading from the apex- used for energizing. If you picture the candle flame, you may see the third spiral.

Contact with indigo ray doesn't need to show itself in any certain gift or guidepost like bending metal. There are some whose indigo energy is of pure being and never is manifested, yet all are aware of such an entity's progress. Others may teach or share in many ways contact with intelligent energy. Others continue in unmanifested form, seeking intelligent infinity. Thus, the manifestation is lesser signpost or evidence than that which is sensed or intuited about a mind/body/spirit complex. Violet-ray beingness is far more indicative of true self.

Session 59: 6-25-1981

At the end of the second major cycle, there were about 345,000 people on Earth 25,000 years ago. In 1981 there was over 4 billion people.

There were three basic divisions of origin of the increase of entities over the past 25,000 years. Firstly, and primarily, those of Maldek, having been able to take up third density once again, were gradually loosed from self-imposed limitations of form.

44

Secondly, there were those of other third-density entrance or neophytes (newcomers) whose vibratory patterns matched the Terran experiential nexus. These then filtered in through incarnative processes.

Thirdly, in approximately the past 200 years has been many Wanderers. All possible opportunities for incarnation are being taken at this time due to harvesting process and the opportunities this offers.

At the beginning of the last 75,000-year period to start third density here on Earth, the transfer has been gradual of souls going from Mars to Earth. (I came from Mars in late 3rd density around 1742 to live my first life here on Earth as a Farmer. My 2nd life was in 1889 as an artist named Bradley and now my 3rd life here on Earth currently.)

Over two billion souls are those of Maldek which have successfully made the transition. (Perhaps about 50% of the population in 1981.)

Approximately 1.9 billion souls have, from many portions of the creation, entered into this experience at various times. The remainder are those who have experienced the first two cycles upon Earth or who have come at some point as Wanderers. Some Wanderers having been on Earth for many thousands of years, others having come far more recently.

The first notion of upward-spiraling light is the scoop, the light energy being scooped in through the attraction of the pyramid shape through the base. Thus, the first configuration is a semi-spiral. This is similar to the vortex you get when you release water from a bathtub, except in the bathtub case the cause is gravitic, whereas in the case of the pyramid, the vortex is that of upward-spiraling light being attracted by the electromagnetic fields engendered by the shape of the pyramid.

The spiral which is used for study and healing begins at or slightly below the Queen's Chamber position, depending upon our Earth and cosmic rhythms. It moves through the King's Chamber position in a sharply delineated (detailed) form and ends at the point whereby the top approximate third of the pyramid may be seen to be intensifying the energy.

The large spiral is drawn into the vortex of the apex of the pyramid. However, some light energy of the more intense nature of red end of spectrum is spiraled once again, causing an enormous strengthening and focusing of energy used for building.

The third complete spiral radiates from the top of the pyramid. It is well to reckon with the foundation semi-spiral which supplies the prana for all that may be affected by the three following upward spirals of light.

The prana scooped in by the pyramid shape gains coherence of energetic direction at the first-spiral zero position. The term "upward-spiraling light" is an indication of that which reaches towards the source of love and light. Thus, all light or prana is upward spiraling, but its direction is unregimented (independent) and not useful for work.

From all points in space, light radiates in our illusion outward in a 360-degree solid angle, and this scoop shape with the pyramid then creates the coherence (unity) to this radiation as a focusing mechanism (machine).

As light is funneled into the zero semi-scoop shape position, as the questioner terms it, it reaches the point of turning. This acts as a compression of the light, multiplying tremendously its coherence (unity) and organization in a spiral one.

There is a transformation across boundaries of dimensions at the start of spiral two, as Don Elkins calls it, much work may be done interdimensionally. There was no chamber at position two in the Giza pyramid.

Position two light spiral is useful only to those whose abilities are capable of serving as conductors of this type of focused spiral. One would not wish to attempt to train third-density entities in such disciplines.

The third spiral radiation from the top of the pyramid is used for energizing. This spiral is extremely full of the positive effects of directed prana (universal energy permeating all entities), and whatever is placed over this shape will receive shocks energizing the electromagnetic fields. This can be most stimulating in third-density applications of mental and bodily configurations. However, if over the pyramid is too long, such shocks may traumatize the entity, such as more than 30 minutes.

Other effects of the pyramid shape beside the spirals: There are several. However, their uses are limited. The use of the resonating chamber position challenges the ability of an adept to face the self. This is one type of mental test which may be used. It is powerful and quite dangerous.

The outer shell of the pyramid shape contains small vortices of light energy which, in the hands of crystallized beings, are useful for various subtle workings upon the healing of invisible bodies affecting the physical body.

Other places are where perfect sleep may be obtained and age reversed. The age reversal position being approximately 5 degrees to 10 degrees above and below the Queens Chamber position in ovoid shapes on each face of the four-sided pyramid, extending into the solid shape approximately one-quarter of the way to the Queen's Chamber position. In other words, it would be just inside the wall of the pyramid a quarter of the way but remained three-quarters from the center at approximately the level above the base of the Queen's Chamber.

Ra: "You must picture the double teardrop extending in both the plane of the pyramid face and in half towards the Queen's Chamber, extending above and below it. You may see this as the

47

position where the light has been scooped into the spiral and then is expanding again. This position is what you may call a prana (life-force) vacuum."

Why this would reverse again: Aging is a function of the effects of various electromagnetic fields upon the electromagnetic fields of the mind/body/spirit complex. In this position there is no input or disturbance of the fields, nor is any activity within the electromagnetic field complex of the mind/body/spirit complex allowed full sway. The vacuum sucks any such disturbance away. Thus, the entity feels nothing and is suspended.

Ra told Don Elkins that the alignment of the pyramid Don built in his yard should be as this resting place for maximum efficacy (the power to create a desired result). Meaning one of the base sides should be aligned 20 degrees east of north. That alignment would be efficacious (effective).

The proper alignment for Earth at this time would be magnetic north. However, specific entities whose energy vortices are more consonant with the true color green orientation would be the 20 degrees east of north.

There are advantages to each orientation. The effect is stronger at magnetic north and can be felt more clearly. The energy, thought weak at 20 degrees east of north coming from the now-distant but soon to be paramount directions is more helpful.

The choice is yours. It is the choice between quantity and quality or wide-band and narrow-band aid in meditation.

There is every indication that when the planetary axis realigns, it will realign 20 degrees east of north to conform to the green vibration. Ra cannot speak of Certainties but are aware that the grosser or less dense materials will be pulled into a conformation with the denser and lighter energies which gives your Logos its proceedings through the realms of experience.

48

Session 60: 7-1-1981

"Energizing shocks" coming from the top of the pyramid come at discrete intervals but come very, very close together in a properly functioning pyramid shape. In one whose dimensions have gone awry, the energy will not be released with regularity or in quanta.

The effect of the Bermuda Triangle is due to a large pyramid beneath the water that releases the third spiral of light in discrete and varying intervals. Entities or craft in the vicinity may change their space/time continuum in some way.

Entities in fifth density or above may tap this energy to communicate information, love, or light across vast distances, but with this energy may be considered trans dimensional leaps. Also, there is the possibility of travel using this formation of energy.

This travel would be instantaneous used primarily by sixth-density entities. As one learns the understandings of discipline of the personality, each of these configurations of prana (universal energy or life-force) is available to the entity without the aid of this shape. One may view the pyramid at Giza as metaphysical training wheels.

The large underwater pyramid off the Florida coast was aided by sixth-density entities of a social memory complex working with Atlanteans prior to Ra working with the Egyptians. Ra also worked with the entities of South America and divided their forces to work within these two cultures.

The pyramid shape was deemed by Ra to be at that time of paramount importance as the physical- training aid for spiritual development. At our current time in evolution of Earth, Ra places little or no emphasis on this shape of the pyramid. It is Ra's honor/duty to attempt to remove the distortions that the use of the pyramid has caused in the thinking of our peoples and in the activities of some of our entities. Ra doesn't deny that such shapes are efficacious (effective), nor do they withhold the general gist of this efficacy (effectiveness). However, Ra wishes to offer their understanding, limited though it is, that contrary to their naïve beliefs many thousand years ago, the optimum shape for initiation does not exist.

Ra: "Let us expand upon this point. When we were aided by sixth-density entities during our own third-density experiences, we, being less bellicose in the extreme, found this teaching to be of help. In our naivete in third density, we had not developed the interrelationships of your barter or money system and power. We were, in fact, a more philosophical third-density planet than your own, and our choices of polarity were much more centered about the understanding of sexual energy transfers and the appropriate relationships between self and other self.

We spent a much larger portion of our space/time working with the unmanifested being. In this less complex atmosphere, it was quite instructive to have this learn/teaching device, and we benefited without the distortions we found occurring among your people.

We have recorded these differences meticulously in the Great Record of Creation that such naivete shall not be necessary again.

At this space/time we may best serve you, we believe, by stating that the pyramid for meditation along with other rounded and arched or pointed circular shapes is of help to you. However, it is our observation that due to the complexity of influences upon the unmanifested being at this space/time nexus among your planetary peoples, it is best that the progress of the mind/body/spirit complex take place without training aids, because when using a training aid, an entity then takes upon itself the Law of Responsibility for the quickened or increased rate of learn/teaching. If this greater understanding is not put into practice in the moment-by-moment experience of the entity, then the usefulness of the training aid becomes negative."

Ra: "The Ark of the Covenant was that place wherein those things most holy, according to the understanding of the one called Moishe, were placed. The article placed therein has been called by your peoples two tablets called the Ten Commandments. There were not two tablets. There was one writing in scroll. This was placed along with the most carefully written accounts by various entities of their beliefs concerning the creation by the One Creator.

The ark was designed to constitute the place wherefrom the priests, as you call those distorted towards the desire to serve their brothers, could draw their power and feel the presence of the One Creator. However, it is to be noted that this entire arrangement was designed not by the one known to the Confederation as Yahweh but rather was designed by negative entities preferring this method of creating an elite called the Sons of Levi."

This was charged with materials it was built with, being given an electromagnetic field. It became an object of power in this way, and, to those whose faith became that untarnished by unrighteousness or separation, this power designed from negativity became positive.

This is in common with each of our orthodox religious systems, which have all become somewhat mixed in orientation (negative and positive) yet offer a pure path to the One Creator which is seen by the pure seeker.

Ra says the Ark of the covenant still exists but they can't state where at to avoid infringement on our peoples by locating. (Recent channeling said it was in Ukraine and that's why it has had destruction in that country).

Unusable heat is generated as Earth moves form third into fourth density. This has to do with the vibrations of third-density having disharmony with fourth density, showing up as physical heating within the Earth.

If an entity is not in harmony with its circumstances, it feels a burning within. The temperature of the physical vehicle does not yet rise, only the heat of the disharmony. However, if an entity persists for a long period in feeling this emotive heat and disharmony, the entire body complex will begin to resonate to this disharmony, and the disharmony will then show up as cancer or other degenerative health distortions.

When an entire planetary system of peoples and cultures repeatedly experiences disharmony on a great scale, the Earth under the feet of these entities shall begin to resonate with the disharmony. Due to the nature of the physical vehicle, disharmony shows up as a blockage of growth or an uncontrolled growth, since the primary function of a mind/body/spirit complex is growth and maintenance. In the case of Earth, the purpose of the planet is the maintenance of orbit and the proper location or orientation with regard to other cosmic influences. In order to have this occurring properly, the interior of Earth is physically hot. Thus, instead of uncontrolled growth you begin to experience uncontrolled heat and its expansive consequences.

Earth is of a honey comb nature. The center is solid and molten.

At one time the Earth had third-density entities living in the honeycomb areas, which is no longer occurring at this present space/time.

There are some inner civilizations or entities living in these areas who do not come and materialize on the Earth's surface at some times. Further, there are some inner-plane entities in Earth which prefer to do some materialization into third density visible in these areas. There are also bases in these areas of those from elsewhere, both positive and negative. There are abandoned cities.

The bases in these areas by those from elsewhere are used for the work of materialization of needed equipment for communication with third-density entities and for resting places

52

for small crafts. They are used for surveillance when it is requested by entities.

Some of the teachers of the Confederation speak partially through these surveillance instruments along computerized lines, and when information is desired and those requesting it are of the proper vibratory level, the Confederation entity itself will then speak.

Many people on Earth request the same basic information in enormous repetition, and for a social memory complex to speak ad infinitum (endlessly) about the need to meditate is a waste of the considerable abilities of such social memory complexes. (I assume we must meditate before asking questions of the Confederation, higher density beings or those who pray to a so-called "God".)

Some entities have been approved by the Council of Saturn the placement and maintenance of these message givers for those who needs are simple, thus reserving the abilities of the Confederation members for those already meditating and absorbing information which are then ready for additional information.

Ra: "We of the Confederation are at the call of those upon your planet. If the call, though sincere, is fairly low in consciousness of the system whereby spiritual evolution may be precipitated (accelerated), then we may only offer that information useful to that particular caller. This is the basic difficulty. Entities receive the basic information about the original thought and the means-that is, meditation and service to others- whereby this Original Thought may be obtained.

Please note that as Confederation members we are speaking for positively oriented entities. We believe the Orion group has precisely the same difficulty.

Once this basic information is received, it is not put into practice in the heart and in the life experience but instead rattles about within the mind complex distortions as would a building block which has lost its place and simply rolls from side to side uselessly, yet still the entity calls. Therefore, the same basic information is repeated. Ultimately the entity decides that it is weary of this repetitive information. However, if an entity puts into practice that which it is given, it will not find repetition except when needed."

Ra can say very little about the distortion of mummification of their designs in constructing the pyramid, for the intent was quite mixed and the uses, though many felt them to be positive, were of a nonpositive order of generation. Ra cannot speak upon this subject without infringement upon some basic energy balances between positive and negative forces upon our planet. Those offering themselves to be mummified thought they were offering themselves in service to others.

The entities that helped Ra use the pyramid shape while Ra was in third density have begun their travel back to the Creator and are no longer experiencing time.

When using the pendulum in discovering energy centers, the weak back-and-forth motion indicates a partial blockage, although not a complete blockage. The strong back-and-forth motion indicates the reverse of blockage, which is over-stimulation of a chakra or energy center, which is occurring in order to attempt to balance some difficulty in body or mind complex activity. This condition is not helpful to the entity, as it is unbalanced.

The groups conscientiousness (diligent in carrying out one's duty to do what is right) is to be recommended.

Session 61: 7-8-1981

Seniority of vibration has reached the green-ray level of vibratory consciousness complexes.

There are four types of cycles given in the moment of entry into incarnation. There are more cosmic and less regularized inpourings which, from time to time affect a sensitized mind/body/spirit complex.

The four rhythms are known on Earth as biorhythms.

There is a fourth cycle called the cycle of gateway of magic of the adept or of spirit. This cycle is completed in approximately 18 of our diurnal (day) cycles.

The cosmic patterns are also a function of the moment of incarnative entrance and have to do with our satellite called the moon, our planets of this galaxy, the galactic sun, and in some cases the instreamings from the major galactic points of energy flow.

The three members of this triad (Don Elkins, Carla and Jim) bring in this energy pattern which is Ra. Ra suggests that it is always of some interest to observe the roadmap, both of the cycles and of the planetary and other cosmic influences, in that one may see certain wide roads or possibilities. However, we remind that this group is a unit.

It was Ra's opinion, that they humbly offer, that each of the group members is in remarkable harmony with each other for this particular third-density illusion at this space/time nexus.

In healing exercises of the body, there's disciplines of the body balancing love and wisdom in the use of the body in its natural functions:

Ra: "I am Ra. We shall speak more briefly than usual due to this instrument's use of the transferred energy. We, therefore, request further queries if our reply is not sufficient.

The body complex has natural functions. Many of these have to do with the unmanifested self and are normally not subject to the need for balancing. There are natural functions which have to do with other self. Among these are touching, love, the sexual life, and those times when the company of another is craved to combat the type of loneliness which is the natural function of the body, as opposed to those types of loneliness which are of the mind/emotion complex or of the spirit.

When these natural functions may be observed in the daily life, they may be examined in order that the love of self and love of other-self verses the wisdom regarding the use of natural functions may be observed. There are many fantasies and stray thoughts which may be examined in most of your people in this balancing process.

Equally to be balance is the withdrawal from the need for these natural functions with regard to other self. On the one hand there is an excess of love. It must be determined whether this is love of self or other self or both. On the other hand, there is an overbalance towards wisdom.

It is well to know the body complex so that it is an ally, balanced and ready to be clearly used as a tool, for each bodily function may be used in higher and higher complexes of energy with other self. No matter what the behavior, the important balancing is the understanding of each interaction on this level with other selves, so that whether the balance may be love/wisdom or wisdom/love, the other self is seen by the self in a balanced configuration, and the self is thus freed for further work."

How feelings affect portions and sensations of the body:

Ra: "It is nearly impossible to speak generally of these mechanisms, for each entity of proper seniority has its own programming. Of the less aware entities we may say that the connection will often seem random, as the Higher Self continues producing catalyst until a bias occurs. In each programmed individual the sensitivities are far more active, and that catalyst not used fully by the mind and spirit is given to the body.

Thus, you may see in this entity the numbing of the arms and the hands, signifying this entity's failure to surrender to the loss of control over the life. Thus, this drama is enacted in the physical distortion complex.

In the questioner (Don) we may see the desire not to be carrying the load it carries given as physical manifestation of the soreness of those muscles for carrying used. That which is truly needed to be carried is a pre-incarnative responsibility, which seems highly inconvenient.

In the case of the scribe, we see a weariness and numbness of feelings ensuing from lack of using catalyst designed to sensitize this entity to quite significant influxes of unfamiliar distortion complexes of the mental, emotional, and spiritual level. As the numbness removes itself from the higher or more responsive complexes, the bodily complex distortions will vanish. This is true also of the other example.

We would note at this time that the totally efficient use of catalyst upon your plane is extremely rare."

Ra could give this information without infringing on free will because each of the group members are already aware of this information. It is interesting to Ra that in many of the queries (questions) Don asks for confirmation rather than information.

Ra: "This is not a dimension of knowing, even subjectively, due to the lack of overview of cosmic and other inpourings which affect each and every situation which produces

57

catalyst. The subjective acceptance of what's at the moment and finding of love within that moment is the greater freedom.

That known as the subjective knowing without proof is, in some degree, a poor friend, for there will be anomalies no matter how much information is garnered due to the distortions which form third density."

Ra: "Within the body there are many polarities which relate to the balancing of the energy centers of the various bodies of the unmanifested entity. It is well to explore these polarities for work in healing. Each entity, of course, a potential polarized portion of an other-self."

The proper balancing exercises for all the sensations of the body:

Ra: "The balancing requires a meditative state in order for the work to be done. However, the balancing of sensation has to do with an analysis of the sensation with especial respect to any unbalanced learning between the love and the wisdom or the positive and the negative. Then whatever is lacking in the balanced sensation is, as in all balancing, allowed to come into the being after the sensation is remembered and recalled in such detail as to overwhelm the senses."

The importance of the appurtenances and other items to be carefully aligned and why just a small ruffle in the sheet by the instrument causes a problem with the reception of Ra:

Ra: "We may attempt an explanation. This contact is narrow band. The instrument is highly sensitive. Thus, we have good entry into it and can use it to an increasingly satisfactory level.

However, the trance condition is not one which is without toll upon this instrument. Therefore, the area above the entrance into the physical complex of this instrument must be kept clear to avoid discomfort to the instrument, especially as it reenters the body complex. The appurtenances give to the instrument's sensory input mental visualizations which aid in the trance beginning. The careful alignment of these is important for the energizing group in that it is a reminder to that support group that it is time for a working. The ritualistic behaviors are triggers for many energies of the support group. You may have noticed more energy being used in workings as the number has increased due to the long-term effect of such ritualistic actions.

This would not aid another group, as it was designed for the particular system of mind/body/spirit complexes and especially the instrument."

The purpose of the frontal lobes of the brain and the conditions necessary for their activation:

Ra: "The frontal lobes of the brain will have much more use in fourth density."

Ra: "The primary mental/emotive condition of this large area of the so-called brain is joy or love in its creative sense. Thus, the energies we have discussed in relationship to the pyramids: all of the healing, the learning, the building, and the energizing are to be found in this area. This is the area tapped by the adept. This is the area which, working through the trunk and root of mind, makes contact with intelligent energy and, through this gateway, intelligent infinity."

Session 62: 7-13-1981

Ra: "The instrument was under specific psychic attack at the time of the beginning of the working (channeling). There was slight irregularity in the (supporting groups) words verbalized in the protective walking the circle. Into this opening came this (negative) entity and began to work upon the instrument now in trance state. This instrument was being quite adversely affected in physical complex distortions. Thus, the circle (of one) was walked. The breath (of the supporting group) of righteousness expelled (forcibly, approximately two and one-half feet above the instrument's head) the thought form, and the circle again walked (by the supporting group around the instrument).

The thought form was of Orion (negative) affiliation. This thought form sought to put an end to this instrument's incarnation by working with the renal (kidney) distortions which, although corrected upon time/space, are vulnerable to one which knows the way to separate time/space molding and space/time distortions which are being unmolded, vulnerable as before the healing."

Ra: "There will be some discomfort. However, we were fortunate this instrument was very open to us and well-tuned. Had we not been able to reach this instrument and instruct you (the supporting group Don and Jim), the instrument's physical vehicle would soon be unviable."

Ra: "We are of the opinion that no lasting harm or distortion will occur."

Ra: "The missed word (from the group vocalizing during the circle of One) was a chance occurrence (by the Orion entity) and not a planned one."

Ra: "...As you begin a working be aware that this instrument is likely being watched for any opportunity. Thus, if the circle is walked with some imperfection, it is well to immediately repeat. The expelling (forcibly) of breath is also appropriate, always to the left."

The expelling of breath being sent above the instrument's head from its right side to its left.

The group was given two spiritual healer names, two allopathic healers that they could see.

The harmonies and loving social intercourse which prevail habitually in this group create a favorable environment for the group to do their work.

This group (Don, Carla and Jim) as all positive channels and supporting groups, is a greatly high priority with the Orion group (negative entities).

The Southern Cross members are of the Orion group. However, those planetary social memory complexes of the Orion constellation have the upper hand and thus rule the other members. In negative thinking, there is always the pecking order and the power against power in separation.

There are fourth and a few fifth-density members of the Orion group. Therefore, the top of the pecking order is fifth density negative.

Earth has some negatively oriented action in sway at this space/time nexus.

Ra: "The early fifth-density negative entity, if oriented towards maintaining cohesion (beings united) as a social memory complex, may in its free will determine that the path to wisdom lies in the manipulation in exquisite (flawless) propriety (conforming) of all other selves. It then, by virtue of its abilities in wisdom, is able to be the leader of forth-density beings which are upon the road to wisdom by exploring the dimensions of love of self and understanding of self. These fifth-density entities see the creation as that which shall be put in order.

Dealing with a plane such as this third density at this harvesting, it will see the mechanism of the call more clearly and have much less distortion towards plunder (forcefully steal) or manipulation by thoughts which are given to negatively oriented entities, although in allowing this to occur and sending less wise entities to do this work, any successes redound (greatly contribute) to the leaders.

The fifth density sees the difficulties posed by the light and in this way directs entities of this vibration to the seeking of targets of opportunity such as this one. If fourth-density temptations, towards distortion of ego etc., are not successful, the fifth-density entity then thinks in terms of the removal of Light."

Ra: "Fifth-density entities are very light beings, although they do have the type of physical vehicle which you understand. Fifth-density entities are very fair to look upon in your standard of beauty.

The thought is what is sent for a fifth-density entity is likely to have mastered this technique or discipline. There is little or no means of perceiving such an entity, for unlike forth-density negative entities, the fifth-density entity walks with light feet.

This instrument was aware of extreme coldness in the past diurnal cycle and spent much more time that your normal attitudes would imagine it be appropriate in what seemed to each of you an extremely warm climate. This was not perceived by the instrument, but the drop in subjective temperature is a sign of presence of a negative or nonpositive or draining entity.

This instrument did mention a feeling of discomfort but was nourished by this group and was able to dismiss it. Had it not been for a random mishap, all would have been well, for you have learned to live in love and light and do not neglect to remember the One Infinite Creator."

It was a fifth-density negative entity that made this particular attack upon the instrument. Which is unusual that a 5th density negative bothered to do this instead of sending a fourth-density negative servant.

Nearly all positive channels and groups may be lessened in their positivity or rendered quite useless by the temptations offered by the fourth-density negative thought forms. They may suggest many distortions towards specific information, toward the

62

aggrandizement (glorification) of the self, towards the flowering of the organization in some political, social, or fiscal way.

These distortions remove the focus from the One Infinite Source of love and light of which we are all messengers, humble and knowing that we are but the tiniest portion of the Creator, a small part of a magnificent entirely of infinite intelligence.

Is there something the group could do to eliminate the problems that the instrument continually experiences of the cold feeling of the psychic attacks?"

Ra: "Yes, you could cease in your attempts to be channels for the love and light of the One Infinite Creator."

Jordyn: "This tells me that if channeling was truly evil, like some religious people like to think, then this positive entity wouldn't be giving an option not to channel anymore if they wanted to. An evil entity, would encourage the channeling to always continue until death, if it was a negative action."

The love and devotion of the group aids the instrument (Carla). Be at peace. There is some toll for this work. This instrument embraces this or Ra could not speak. Rest then in that peace and love and do as you will, as you wish, as you feel. Let there be an end to worry when this is accomplished. The great healer of distortions is love.

First density is composed of core atomic vibrations that are in the red spectrum, the second in orange, ect.

The core vibrations of our planet are still in the red and the second-density beings are still in orange at this space/time right now, and each density as it exists on our planet right now has a different core vibration.

Ra: "You must see Earth as being seven Earths. There is red, orange, yellow, and there will soon be a completed green-

63

color vibratory locus for fourth-density entities which they will call Earth. During the fourth-density experience, due to lack of development of fourth-density entities, the third-density planetary sphere is not useful for habitation, since the early fourth-density entity will not know precisely how to maintain the illusion that fourth density cannot be seen or determined from any instrumentation available to any third density.

Thus, in fourth density the red, orange, and green energy nexi of your planet will be activated while the yellow is in potentiation along with blue and indigo."

Jordyn: "I assume this means first, second and fourth density entities will be upon Earth during fourth density New Earth. Third density entities will no longer be habitable and thus, third density entities that did not make the fourth density harvest in approximately 2030 will be transferred to a third density planet to continue their learning and evolution as there is no judgement for the polarity chosen. The 4th density positive can be considered Heaven, while the 4th density negative planet may be considered as Hell."

SESSION 63: 7-18-1981

When the instrument goes to the restroom several times before or after a session, this is due to the elimination of the distortion leavings of the material which Ra uses for contact. This occurs variably, sometimes beginning before contact, other workings this occurring after the contact.

Ra: "The body complex is distorted due to psychic attack in the area of the kidneys and urinary tract. There is also distortion continuing due to arthritis. You may expect this psychic attack to be constant, as this instrument has been under observation by negatively oriented force for some time."

How to lessen the effectiveness of psychic attacks?

Ra: "Continue in love and praise and thanksgiving to the Creator. Examine previous material. Love is the great protector.

Vital energy is the complex of energy levels of mind, body and spirit. Unlike physical energy, it requires the integrated complexes vibrating in a useful manner.

The faculty of will can, to a variable extent, replace missing vital energy, and this has occurred in past workings in this instrument. This is not recommended. At this time the vital energies are well nourished in mind and spirit, although the physical energy level is low at this time.

Vital energy is a function of the awareness or bias of the entity with respect to his polarity or general unity with the Creator or creation.

Ra: "The vital energy may be seen to be that deep love of life or life experiences such as the beauty of creation and the appreciation of other selves and the distortions of your co-Creator's making which are of beauty.

Without this vital energy, the least distorted physical complex will fail and perish. With this love or vital energy or elan (enthusiastic energy), the entity may continue though the physical complex is greatly distorted."

Ra: "It is misleading to speak of gains and losses when dealing with the subject of the cycle's ending and the green-ray cycle beginning upon your sphere. It is to be kept in the forefront of the faculties of intelligence that there is one creation in which there is no loss. There are progressive cycles for experiential use by entities.

As the green-ray cycle or the density of love and understanding begins to take shape, the yellow-ray plane or Earth which you now enjoy in your dance will cease to be inhabited for some period of your space/time as the space/time necessary for fourth-density entities to learn their ability to shield their density from that of third is learned. After this period there will come a time when third density may again cycle on the yellow-ray sphere.

Meanwhile there is another sphere, congruent to a great extent with yellow ray, forming. This fourth-density sphere coexists with first, second, and third. It is of a denser nature due to the rotational core atomic aspects of its material. We (Ra states) have discussed this subject with you.

The fourth-density entities which incarnate at this space/time are fourth density in the view of experience but are incarnating in less dense vehicles due to desire to experience and aid in the birth of fourth density upon this plane.

You may note that fourth-density entities have a great abundance of compassion."

At present we have, in third-density incarnation on this plane, those third-density entities of the planet Earth who have been here for some number of incarnations who will graduate in the three-way split, either positive polarity harvested entities remaining in this planetary influence but not upon this plane, the negative polarity harvestable going to a fourth density negative planet, and the rest unharvestable third density going to another third-density planet. In addition to these entities, we have some already harvestable from other third-density planets who have come here and have incarnated in third-density form to make transition with this planet into fourth density. There are also approximately 65 million Wanderers in 1981.

The recent phenomenon of third-density harvestable entities from other planets incarnating here for fourth-density experience is not yet in excess of 35,000 entities. These entities are incarnating with a double body in activation. The entities birthing these fourth-density entities experience a great feeling of the connection and the use of spiritual energies during pregnancy. This is due to the necessity for manifesting the double body.

66

This transitional body will be able to appreciate fourth-density vibratory complexes as the instreaming increases without the disruption of the third-density body. If a third-density entity were electrically aware of fourth density in full, the third-density electrical fields would fail due to incompatibility. These entities will die according to third-density necessities.

The third and fourth, combination, density's body will die according to other necessity of third-density mind/body/spirit complex distortions.

The purpose of the combined activation of mind/body/spirit complexes is that they are, to some extent, consciously aware of those fourth-density understandings which third density is unable to remember due to the forgetting. Thus fourth-density is unable to remember due to the forgetting. Thus, fourth-density experience may be begun with the added attraction to an entity oriented toward service to others of dwelling in a troubled third-density environment and offering its love and compassion.

The purpose in transition to earth prior to the complete changeover is for the experience to be gained here before the harvesting process. These entities are not Wanderers in the sense that this planetary sphere is their fourth-density home planet. However, the experience for this service is earned only by those harvested third-density entities which have demonstrated a great deal of orientation towards service to others. It is a privilege to be allowed this clearly in incarnation, and there is much experiential catalyst in service to other selves at this harvesting.

Some children in the dual activated bodies have demonstrated the ability to bend metal mentally, which is a fourth-density phenomenon. The reason they can do this and the fifth-density Wanderers here on Earth cannot do it, is the fact that they have the fourth-density body in activation. Since Wanderers are third density activated in mind/body/spirit and are subject to the

67

forgetting, which can only be penetrated with disciplined meditation and working.

Harvestable third density entities who very recently have been coming here are coming here late enough so that they will not affect the polarization through their teachings. They are not infringing upon the first distortion of free will because they are children now, and they won't be old enough to really affect any of the polarization until the transition is well advanced. However, the Wanderers who have come here are older and have a greater ability to affect polarization. They must do their affecting as a function of their ability to penetrate the forgetting process in order to be within free will.

Some of the harvestable third-density entities who can bend metal are over fifty years old and some over thirty.

Any entity who, by accident or by careful design, penetrates intelligent energy's gateway may use the shaping powers of this energy. (such as bending metal).

Now as this transition continues into fourth-density activation; in order to inhabit this fourth-density sphere it will be necessary for all third-density physical bodies to go through the process we refer to as death. There are people at this time on this fourth density planet who have already gone through this process, only in the very recent past; this population is from other planets since the harvesting has not yet occurred on Earth yet. It is from planets where the harvesting has already occurred. These entities are in dual bodies at this time.

As the fourth-density sphere is activated, there is heat energy being generated. This heat energy is generated on the third-density sphere only. The experiential distortions of each dimension are discrete.

At this time cosmic influxes (inflows) are conducive (helpful) to true color green core particles being formed and material of this nature being formed. However, there is a mixture of the yellow-ray and green-ray environments at this time, necessitating the birthing of transitional mind/body/spirit complex types of energy distortions.

At full activation of the true color green density of love, the planetary sphere will be solid and inhabitable upon its own, and the birthing that takes place will have been transformed through the process of time to the appropriate type of vehicle to appreciate in full the fourth-density planetary environment. At this nexus the green-ray environment exists to a far greater extent in time/space than in space/time.

As our planet is spiraled by the spiraling action of the entire major galaxy and our planetary system spirals into the new position, the fourth-density vibrations becoming more and more pronounced. These atomic core vibrations begin to create the fourth-density sphere and gradually create green-ray-density bodily complexes. This will take place beginning with our third-density type of physical vehicle and, through the means of bisexual reproduction, become by evolutionary processes the fourth-density body complexes.

(Essentially, third-density mothers with dual activated bodies giving birth will give birth to fourth density babies.)

The influxes of true color green energy complexes will more and more create the conditions where the atomic structure of cells of bodily complexes is that of the density of love. The entities inhabiting these physical vehicles will be, to some extent, fourth density babies born and as harvest is completed, the harvested entities of this planetary influence.

There is a three-dimensional clock-face or spiral of endlessness associated with the entire major galaxy so that as it revolves it carries all of these stars and planetary systems through transitions from density to density, which is planned by the Logos.

The Logos did not plan for the core heating effect in our third-density transition into fourth, except for the condition of free will, which is planned by the Logos as it, itself, is a creature of free will. In this climate an infinity of events or conditions may occur. They cannot be said to be planned by the Logos but can be said to have been freely allowed.

The spiritual configuration as well as mental biases of people on Earth has been responsible for the body complex distortions of the planetary sphere.

When third density goes out of activation and into potentiation, Earth will then be a planet that is first, second, and fourth density. There will be no activated third-density vibrations on this planet, which are the mind/body/spirit complexes of third density, artifacts, thought forms and feelings which these co-Creators have produced. This is third density.

Session 64: 7-26-1981

The cause of the instrument's transitory vital energy distortion, which lessens the free flow of vital energy, is a bias towards the yearning for expression of devotion to the One Creator in group worship.

Ra: "This entity was yearning for this protection both consciously in that it responds to the accoutrements (accessories or equipment) of this expression, the ritual, the colors, and their meanings as given by the distortion system of the church, the song of praise, and the combined prayers of thanksgiving and, most of all, that which may be seen to be most centrally magical, the intake of that food which is not of this dimension but has been transmuted into metaphysical nourishment in what this distortion of expression calls the holy communion.

The subconscious reason, it being the stronger for this yearning, was the awareness that such expression is, when appreciated by an entity as the transmutation into the presence of the One Creator, a great protection of the entity as it moves in the path of service to others.

The principle behind any ritual of the white magical nature is to so configure the stimuli which reach down into the trunk of mind that this arrangement causes the generation of disciplined and purified emotion or love which then maybe both protection and the key to the gateway to intelligent infinity."

Why a slight error made in the ritual starting this communication allowed the intrusion by an Orion entity?

Ra: "I am Ra. This contact is narrow band and its preconditions precise. The other-self offering its service in the negative path also is possessed of the skill of the swordsman. You deal in this contact with forces of great intensity poured into a vessel as delicate as a snowflake and as crystalline.

The smallest of lapses may disturb the regularity of this pattern of energies which forms the channel for these transmissions.

We may note for your information that our pause was due to the necessity of being quite sure that the mind/body/spirit complex of the instrument was safely in the proper light configuration or density before we dealt with the situation. Far better would it be to allow the shell to become unviable than to allow the mind/body/spirit complex to be misplaced."

Rituals or techniques used by Ra in seeking in the direction of service:

Ra: "I am Ra. To speak of that which sixth-density social memory complexes labor within in order to advance is at best misprision (neglect/failure) of plain communication, for much is lost in transmission of concept from density to density, and the discussion of sixth density is inevitably distorted greatly.

However, we shall attempt to speak to your query, for it is a helpful one in that it allows us to express once again the total unity of creation. We seek the Creator upon a level of shared experience to which you are not privy (knowledgeable of the secret information), and rather than surrounding ourselves in light, we have become light. Our understanding is that there is no other material except light. Our rituals, are an infinitely subtle continuation of the balancing processes which you are now beginning to experience.

We seek now without polarity. Thus, we do not invoke any power from without, for our search has become internalized as we become light/love and love/light. These are the balances we seek, the balances between compassion and wisdom which more and more allow our understanding of experience to be informed that we may come closer to the unity with the One Creator which we so joyfully seek.

Your rituals at your level of progress contain the concept of polarization, and this is most central at your particular space/time."

Ra can't answer the query as to the techniques Ra used in third density to evolve in mind, body and spirit. That query lies beyond the Law of Confusion (Free will), as does their fourth-density experience.

Ra: "Let us express a thought. Ra is not elite. To speak of our specific experiences to a group which honors us is to guide to the point of a specific advising. Our work was that of your people, of experiencing the catalyst of joys and sorrow. Our circumstances were somewhat more harmonious. Let it be said that any entity or group may create the most splendid harmony in any outer atmosphere. Ra's experiences are no more than your own. Yours is that dance at this space/time in third-density harvest."

Any words upon the particular subject of possible records left near, in, or under the Great Pyramid at Giza creates the

72

possibility of infringement upon free will. Therefore, Ra cannot answer.

The gateway of magic for the adept occurring in 18-day cycles:

Ra: "I am Ra. The mind/body/spirit complex is born under a series of influences, both lunar, planetary, cosmic, and in some cases, karmic. The moment of the birthing into this illusion begins the cycles we have mentioned.

The spiritual or adept's cycle is an eighteen-day cycle and operates with the equalities of the sine wave. Thus, there are a few excellent days on the positive side of the curve, that being the first nine days of the cycle- precisely the fourth, the fifth, and the sixth- when workings are most appropriately undertaken, given that the entity is still without total conscious control of its mind/body/spirit distortion/reality.

The most interesting portion of this information, like that of each cycle, is the noting of the critical point wherein passing from the ninth to the tenth and from the eighteenth to the first days the adept will experience some difficulty especially when there is a transition occurring in another cycle at the same time. At the nadir (lowest point) of each cycle the adept will be at its least powerful but will not be open to difficulties in nearly the degree that it experiences at critical time."

The day the infant was born starts the 18-day cycles, continuing it through the life. It is not necessary to identify the instant of birth, but the day of birth is satisfactory for all but the finest workings.

This cycle is a helpful tool to the adept, but as the adept becomes more balanced, the workings designed will be dependent less and less upon these cycles of opportunity and more and more even in their efficacy (desire to produce an intended result).

73

Ra is fettered (restrained) from speaking specifically about the level of abilities the adept would reach in order to be independent of the cyclical tool. This is due to the group's work, so to speak would seem to judge. However, this cycle is in the same light as the astrological balances within the group; that is, they are interesting but not critical.

Recent research indicated that the normal sleep cycle for entities on earth occurs one hour later each diurnal period, so that we have a twenty-five-hour cycle instead of twenty-four: In some cases, this is correct. The planetary influences from those of Mars experience memory have some effect on these third-density physical bodily complexes. Mars race has given its genetic material to many bodies upon this plane.

What is the value of modern medical techniques in respect to Karma?

Ra: "...For that which is allopathic among your healing practices is somewhat two-sided.

Firstly, you must see the possibility/probability that each and every allopathic healer is in fact a healer. Within your cultural nexus, this training is considered the appropriate means of perfecting the healing ability. In the most basic sense, any allopathic healer may be seen to, perhaps, be one whose desire is service to others in alleviation of bodily complex and mental/emotional complex distortions so that the entity to be healed may experience further catalyst over a longer period of life. This is a great service to others when appropriate due to the accumulation of distortions toward wisdom and love which can be created through the use of the space/time continuum of your illusion.

In observing the allopathic concept of the body complex as a machine, we may note the symptomology (symptoms of the society) of a societal complex seemingly dedicated to the most intransigent (uncompromising) desire for the distortions of

74

distraction, anonymity (being anonymous), and sleep. This is the result rather than the cause of societal thinking upon your plane.

In turn this mechanical concept of the body complex has created the continuing proliferation (rapid increase) of distortions towards what you would call ill health, due to the strong chemicals used to control and hide bodily distortions. There is a realization among many of your people that there are more efficacious (effective) systems of healing not excluding the allopathic but also including the many other avenues of healing."

Seeking allopathic aid for a bodily distortion vs. experiencing the catalyst and not correcting the distortion:

Ra: "If the entity is polarized towards service to others, analysis properly proceeds along the lines of consideration of which path offers the most opportunity for service to others.

For the negatively polarized entity, the antithesis (opposite) is the case.

For the unpolarized entity, the considerations are random and most likely in the direction towards comfort."

A four-toed Bigfoot cast shown to Don Elkins by somebody he knows was an entity of a small group of thought forms.

There weren't any Bigfoot remains found after the entities have died on our surface. Ra then suggested that exploration of the caves underlining some of the western coastal mountain regions of North America will one day offer such remains. They will not be generally understood if this culture survives in its present form long enough for this probability/possibility vortex to occur.

How to examine the sensations of the body during healing exercises?

75

Humans are already experiencing sensations.

Ra: "Most of these sensations or nearly all of them are transient (short lived) and without interest. However, the body is the creature of the mind. Certain sensations carry importance due to the charge or power which is felt by the mind upon the experience of this sensation.

For instance, at this space/time nexus, one sensation is carrying a powerful charge and may be examined. This is the sensation of what you call the distortion towards discomfort due to the cramped position of the body complex during this working. In balancing you would then explore this sensation. Why is this sensation powerful? Because it was chosen in order that the entity might be of service to others in energizing this contact.

Each sensation that leaves the aftertaste of meaning upon the mind, that leaves the taste within the memory, shall be examined. These are the sensations of which we speak."

Session 65: 8-8-1981

More entities may increase in their seeking in the near future on this Earth. The generalities of expression can never be completely correct. However, when faced with a hole in current belief systems, an entity's eyes may peer through the hole for the first time to more accurate facts. This tendency is probably given the possibility/probability vortices within our space/time and time/space continua at this nexus.

The intention Wanderers had prior to incarnation here on Earth at this time was them finding it a privilege of the opportunity to be more fully of service because of the increased seeking (of third-density entities on Earth). There are many Wanderers who dysfunction with regard to the planetary ways of our peoples have caused, to some extent, a condition of being caught up in a configuration of mind complex activity which may prohibit the intended service.

Ra was speaking slower when attempting to channel even more narrow band than before, when the instrument became somewhat weak and more fragile than usual, including a continuing pain which has a weakening effect on physical energy.

Seniority by vibration of incarnation has greatly polarized those upon the surface of the planet now, and the influx in Wanderers has greatly increased the mental configuration towards things of a more spiritual nature.

Kathryn Jordyn: "I have seniority of vibration at 87% positive polarity. This also means I'm a part of the 65% of Earth entities harvestable for fourth-density positive New Earth."

So, seniority by vibration entities and the influx of Wanderers are one of the factors creating a better atmosphere for service.

The paranormal events occurring are not designed to increase seeking but are manifestations of those whose vibratory configuration enables these entities to contact the gateway to intelligent infinity. These entities capable of paranormal service may determine to be of such service on a conscious level. This, however, is a function of the entity and its free will and not the paranormal ability.

The greater opportunity for service due to the many Earth changes as we progress into fourth density, such as the healing effect and the ability of people to perform paranormal activities, offers many challenges, difficulties and seeming distresses within our illusion to many who will seek to understand the reason for the malfunctioning of the physical rhythms of their planet.

Moreover, there exist probability/possibility vortices which spiral towards your bellicose (war-like) actions. Many of these vortices are not of the nuclear war but of the less annihilatory (lethal) but more lengthy "conventional" war. This situation, if

77

formed in our illusion, would offer many opportunities for seeking and for service.

Ra: "I am Ra. The possibility/probabilities exist for situation in which great portions of your continent and the globe in general might be involved in the type of warfare which you might liken to guerrilla warfare (small, independent groups using irregular tactics to fight against larger forces). The ideal of freedom from the so-called invading force of either the controlled fascism (far-right authoritarian) or the equally controlled social common ownership of all things would stimulate great quantities of contemplation upon the great polarization implicit in the contrast between freedom and control. In this scenario which is being considered at this time/space nexus, the idea of obliterating valuable sites and personnel would not be considered a useful one. Other weapons would be used which do not destroy as your nuclear arms would. In this ongoing struggle, the light of freedom would burn within the mind/body/spirit complexes capable of such polarization. Lacking the opportunity for overt (open in plain sight) expression of the love of freedom, the seeking for inner knowledge would take root aided by those of the Brothers and Sisters of Sorrow which remember their calling upon this sphere."

What is the value of Edgar Cayce's prophecies with respect to the many Earth changes he mentioned?

Ra: "I am Ra. Consider the shopper entering the store to purchase food with which to furnish the table for the time period you call a week. Some stores have some items, others a variant set of offerings. We speak of these possibility/probability vortices when asked with the understanding that such are as a can, jar, or portion of good in your store.

It is unknown to us as we scan your time/space whether your people will shop hither or yon. We can only name some of the items available for the choosing. The record which the one you call Edgar read from is useful in that same manner. There is less knowledge in this material of other possibility/probability vortices

78

and more attention paid to the strongest vortex. We see the same vortex but also see many others. Edgar's material could be likened unto one hundred boxes of your cold cereal, another vortex likened unto three, or six, or fifty of another product which is eaten by your peoples for breakfast. That you will breakfast is close to certain. The menu is your own choosing.

The value of prophecy must be realized to be only that of expressing (the most likely) possibilities. Moreover, it must be, in our humble opinion, carefully taken into consideration that any time/space viewing, whether by one of your time/space viewing or by one such as we who view the time/space from a dimension, exterior to it will have a quite difficult time expressing time measurement values. Thus, prophecy given in specific terms is more interesting for the content or type of possibility predicted than for the space/time nexus of its supposed occurrence."

Given the amount of strength of the possibility/probability vortex which posits the expression by the planet itself of the difficult birthing of the planetary self into fourth density, it would be greatly surprising were not many who have some access to space/time able to perceive this vortex.

Kathryn: "I have prophecy as well and can see things that will happen in the future. I have videos on my YouTube channel showing proof of 32 dreams of the future actually coming true or at times a thought coming to my head that actually came true in the future."

The amount of this cold cereal in the grocery, to use Ra's analogy, is disproportionately large. Each which prophesies does so from a unique level, position, or vibratory configuration. Thus, biases and distortions will accompany much prophecy.

It was the aim of Wanderers to serve the entities of this planet in whatever way was requested, and it was also their aim that their vibratory patterns might lighten the planetary vibration as a whole, thus ameliorating (improving) the effects of planetary disharmony and palliating (lighten) any results of this disharmony.

Specific intentions such as aiding in a situation not yet manifest, such as the future, are not the aim of Wanderers. Light and love go where they are sought and needed, and their direction is not planned aforetime (in the past).

Each of the Wanderers acts as a function of the biases he has developed in any way he sees fit to communicate or simply be in his polarity to aid the total consciousness of the planet. The physical presence of Wanderers does aid the planet.

Ra: "You may, at this time, note that as with any entities, each Wanderer has its unique abilities, biases, and specialties, so that from each portion of each density represented among the Wanderers come an array of pre-incarnative talents which then may be expressed upon this plane which you now experience, so that each Wanderer, in offering itself before incarnation, has some special service to offer in addition to the doubling effect of planetary love and light and the basic function of serving as beacon or shepherd.

Thus, there are those of fifth density whose abilities to express wisdom are great. There are fourth- and sixth-density Wanderers whose ability to serve as passive radiators or broadcasters of love and love/light are immense. There are many others whose talents brought into this density are quite varied.

Thus, Wanderers have three basic functions once the forgetting is penetrated, the first two being basic, the tertiary (third) one being unique to that particular mind/body/spirit complex.

We may not at this point while you ponder the possibility/probability vortices that although you have many, many items which cause distress and thus offer seeking and service opportunities, there is always one container in that store of peace, love, light, and joy. This vortex may be very small, but to turn one's back upon it is to forget the infinite possibilities of the present moment. Could your planet polarize towards harmony in one fine, strong moment of inspiration? Yes, my friends. It is not probable, but it is ever possible."

Among planetary harvest which yield a harvest of mind/body/spirit complexes, approximately 10 percent are negative, approximately 60 percent are positive, and approximately 30 percent are mixed, with nearly all harvest being positive. In the event of mixed harvest, it is almost unknown for the majority of the harvest to be negative. When a planet moves strongly towards the negative, there is almost no opportunity for harvestable positive polarization, because the ability to polarize positively requires a certain degree of self-determination.

Jordyn: "In a channeling session my higher-self in sixth density positive stated that 65% are positively oriented on Earth currently as of 2023. That leaves 35% being either negatively harvestable or mixed. Being at least 95% negative can make an entity harvestable for the 4th density negative planet. Those mixed will continue their evolutionary journey on another 3rd density planet after Earth fully activates fourth-density into the New Earth at the Harvest."

In a mixed harvest, there is nearly always disharmony and, therefore, added catalyst in the form of "Earth changes" at the end of a harvesting period.

It is the Confederation's desire to serve those who may indeed seek more intensely because of this added catalyst.

Ra doesn't choose to attempt to project the success of added numbers to the harvest, for this would not be appropriate. Ra stated that they are servants. If they are called, they will serve with all their strength. To count the added harvestable numbers is without virtue (showing high moral standards/ethical).

The added catalyst at the end of the cycle is a function specifically of the orientation of the consciousness that inhabits the planet. The consciousness has provided the catalyst for itself in orienting its thinking in the way it has oriented it, thus acting upon itself the same as catalyst of bodily pain and disease act upon the single mind/body/spirit complex. The planet may be seen as a planetary entity as somewhat of a single entity made up of billions of mind/body/spirit complexes.

This entity has not yet formed a social memory but is yet a single entity just as one of us can be called a single entity. Just as one can look at a single sun as an entity, a galaxy with billions of stars as an entity, and the entire universe of galaxies as a single entity in this octave of our existence with 250 billion suns in our universe.

Ra: "Let us attempt to speak upon this interesting subject. In your space/time, you and your peoples are the parents of that which is in the womb. The Earth is ready to be born, and the delivery is not going smoothly. When this entity has become born, it will be instinct with the social memory complex of its parents which have become fourth-density positive. In this density there is a broader view.

You may begin to see your relationship to the Logos or sun with which you are most intimately associated. This is not the relationship of parent to child but of Creator, that is Logos, to Creator that is the mind/body/spirit complex, as Logos. When this realization occurs, you may then widen the field of "eyeshot," infinitely recognizing parts of the Logos throughout the one infinite creation and feeling, with the roots of mind informing the intuition, the parents aiding their planets in evolution in reaches vast and unknown in the creation, for this process occurs many, many times in the evolution of the creation as a whole."

Why the Wanderer goes through the forgetting process?

Ra: "The reason is twofold. First, the genetic properties of the connection between the mind/body/spirit complex and the cellular structure of the body is different for third density than for third/fourth density.

Secondly, the free will of third-density entities needs be preserved. Thus, Wanderers volunteer for third-density genetic or DNA connections to the mind/body/spirit complex. The forgetting process can be penetrated to the extent of the Wanderer remembering what it is and why it is upon the planetary sphere. However, it would be an infringement if Wanderers penetrate the forgetting so far as to activate the more dense bodies and thus be able to live in a godlike manner. This would not be proper for those who have chosen to serve.

The new fourth-density entities which are becoming able to demonstrate various newer abilities are doing so as a result of the present experience, not as a result of memory. There are always a few exceptions, and we ask your forgiveness for constant barrages (bombardment) of over-generalization."

The resonating chamber in the pyramids was used so the adept could meet the self.

One meets the self in the center or deeps of the being. The resonating chamber may be likened unto the symbology of the burial and resurrection of the body, wherein the entity dies to self and, through this confrontation of apparent loss and realization of essential gain, is transmuted into a new risen being. This apparent death of losing the desires that are illusory, common desire of third density and gaining desire of total service to others.

Kathryn: "I believe this is what the Bible meant when it said that one must die to itself to be born again."

This was the purpose and intent of the chamber, as well as forming a necessary portion of the King's Chamber position effectiveness.

This chamber worked upon the mind and the body to create this awareness in him of dying to the desires of third density and resurrecting to the desires of total service to others. This mind was affected by sensory deprivation and the archetypical reactions to being buried alive with no possibility of extricating (freeing) the self (from a constraint). The body was affected both by the mind configuration and by the electrical and piezoelectrical properties of the materials (that allows the materials to absorb mechanical energy from its surroundings of vibration into electrical energy that can power other devices.) This was used in the construction of the resonating chamber.

Session 66: 8-12-1981

The crystallized healer is analogous (has many similarities, but belongs to different categories) to the pyramidal action of the King's Chamber position.

Ra: "The energy which is used is brought into the field complex of the healer by the outstretched hand used in a polarized sense. However, this energy circulates through the various points of energy to the base of the spine and, to a certain extent, the feet, thus coming through the main energy centers of the healer, spiraling through the feet, turning at the red energy center towards a spiral at the yellow energy center, and passing through the green energy center in a microcosm (miniature version) of the King's Chamber energy configuration of prana (cosmic energy or life-force energy); this then continuing for the third spiral through the blue energy center and being sent therefrom through the gateway back to intelligent infinity.

It is from the green center that the healing prana moves into the polarized healing right hand and therefrom to the one to be healed.

We may note that there are some who use the yellow-ray configuration to transfer energy, and this may be done, but the effects are questionable and, with regard to the relationship between the healer, the healing energy, and the seeker, questionable due to the propensity (tendency) for the seeker to continue requiring such energy transfers without any true healing taking place in the absence of the healer due to the lack of penetration of the armoring shell of which you spoke."

A Wanderer who has an origin from fifth or sixth density can attempt such healings and have little or no results.

Ra: "You may see the Wanderer as the infant attempting to verbalize the sound complexes of your people's. The memory of the ability to communicate is within the infant's undeveloped mind complex, but the ability to practice or manifest this, called speech, is not immediately forth coming due to the limitations of the mind/body/spirit complex it has chosen to be a part of in this experience.

So it is with the Wanderer, which, remembering the ease with which adjustments can be made in the home density, yet still having entered third density, cannot manifest that memory due to the limitation of the chosen experience. The chances of the Wanderer being able to heal in third density are only more than those native to this density because the desire to serve may be stronger and this method of service chosen."

The dual activated, third and fourth density, bodies harvested from other third-density planets are able to heal using these techniques, but as beginners of fourth density, the desire may not be present.

A Wanderer may have the desire to learn the techniques of healing while being trapped in a third density body. He then may be primarily concerned with the balancing and unblocking of energy centers. Only if a healer has become balanced may it be a channel for the balancing of an other-self. The healing is first practiced upon the self.

85

The role of a healer is to offer an opportunity for realignment or aid in realignment of either energy centers or some connection between the energies of mind and body, spirit and mind, or spirit and body. This latter is very rare. The seeker will then have a reciprocal (done in return) opportunity to accept a novel (new perspective) view of the self, a variant arrangement of patterns of energy influx. If the entity, at any level, desires to remain in the configuration of distortion which seems to need healing, it will do so. If, upon the other hand, the seeker chooses the novel configuration, it is done through free will.

This is one great difficulty with other forms of energy transfer in that they do not carry through the process of free will, as this process is not native to yellow ray.

The difference between someone healing themselves through mental configuration and being healed by a healer is that the healer does not heal. The crystallized healer is a channel for intelligent energy which offers an opportunity to an entity that it might help them heal itself.

In no case is there another description of healing.

Therefore, there is no difference as long as the healer never approaches one whose request for aid has not come to it previously. This is also true of the more conventional healers of your culture, and if these healers could but fully realize that they are responsible only for offering the opportunity of healing, and not for the healing, many of these entities would feel an enormous load of misconceived responsibility fall from them.

A mind/body/spirit complex in some cases would be seeking a source of gathered and focused light energy. This source could be another mind/body/spirit complex sufficiently crystallized for this purpose of the pyramid shape or something else.

86

Perhaps the greatest healer is within the self and may be tapped with continued meditation. The many forms of healing available to our peoples... each have virtue and may be deemed appropriate by any seeker who wishes to alter the physical body distortions or some connection between the various portions of the mind/body/spirit complex.

Psychic surgery:

There's psychic surgery in the Philippine Islands. The psychic surgeon (healer) provides a training aid or a way of creating a reconfiguration of the mind of the patient to be healed as the patient observes the action of the healer in seeing the materialized blood ect. And reconfigures the roots of mind to believe the healing is done, and, therefore, heals himself.

Ra: "There are times when the malcondition to be altered is without emotional, mental, or spiritual interest to the entity and is merely that which has, perhaps by chance genetic arrangement, occurred. In these cases, that which is apparently dematerialized will remain dematerialized and may be observed as so by any observer. The malcondition which has an emotional, mental, or spiritual charge is likely not to remain dematerialized in the sense of the showing of the objective referent (important) to an observer. However, if the opportunity has been taken by the seeker, the apparent malcondition of the physical complex (body) will be at variance (discrepancy) with the actual health of the seeker and the lack of experiencing the distortions which the objective referent would suggest still held sway.

For instance, in this instrument (Carla) the removal of three small cysts was the removal of material having no interest to the entity. Thus, these growths remained dematerialized after the so-called psychic surgery experience. In other psychic surgery, the kidneys of this instrument were carefully offered a new configuration of beingness which the entity embraced. However, this particular portion of the mind/body/spirit complex carried a great deal of emotional, mental and spiritual charge due to this

87

distorted functioning being the cause of great illness in a certain configuration of events which culminated in this entity's conscious decision to be of service. Therefore, any objective scanning of this entity's renal (kidney) complex would indicate the rather extreme dysfunctional aspect which is showed previous to the psychic surgery experience.

The key is not in the continuation of the dematerialization of distortion to the eye of the beholder but rather lies in the choosing of the newly materialized configuration which exists in time/space. (metaphysical)

Ra: "I am Ra. Healing is done in the time/space (metaphysical) portion of the mind/body/spirit complex, is adopted by the form-making or etheric body, and is then given to the space/time physical illusion for use in the activated yellow mind/body/spirit complex. It is the adoption of the configuration health by the etheric body in time/space which is the key to what you call health, not any event which occurs in space/time. In the process you may see the transdimensional aspect of will, for it is the will, the seeking, the desire of the entity which causes the indigo body to use the novel (new) configuration and to reform the body which exists in space/time (the physical). This is done in an instant and may be said to operate without regard to time. We may note that in the healing of very young children, there is often an apparent healing by the healer in which the young entity has no part. This is never so, for the mind/body/spirit complex in time/space is always capable of willing the distortions it choses for experience, no matter what the apparent age of the entity."

The desire and will that operate through to the transdimensional time/space section is an activity of the Creator. The crystallized healer has no will. It offers an opportunity without attachment to the outcome, for it is aware that all is one and that the Creator is knowing Itself.

An entity may consciously desire healing greatly within the being, at some level, find some cause where certain configurations that seem quite distorted are, in fact, at that level, considered appropriate. The reason for assuming these distortions appropriate would be that these distortions would aid the entity in reaching its ultimate objective in the path of evolutions towards its desired polarity.

There is often a complex reason for the programming of a distorted physical complex pattern, even though the distortion may appear to interfere with further service to others, if that's what the entity chose for their polarization. In any case, mediation is always an aid to knowing the self.

A vertical position of the spine is somewhat helpful in the meditative procedure.

Each unmanifested self is unique. The basic polarities within the body have to do with the balanced vibratory rates between the first three energy centers and, to a lesser extent, each of the other energy centers.

As Ra mentioned before, there is an energizing spiral emitted from the top of any pyramid and that people could benefit by placing this under the head for 30 minutes or less. The vibration offered by the energizing spiral of the pyramid is such that each cell, both in space/time (physical) and time/space (non-physical), is charged as if hooked to our electricity. The keenness of mind, the physical and sexual energy of body, and the attunement of will of spirit are all touched by this energizing influence. It may be used in any of these ways. It is possible to overcharge a battery, and this is the cause of Ra's cautioning any who use such pyramidal energies to remove the pyramid after a charge has been received. (30 minutes or less).

There are also substances which you may ingest that cause the body to experience an increase of energy. These substances are crude, working rather roughly upon the body increasing the flow of adrenalin.

The small pyramid shall have the appropriate proportions to develop the spirals in the Giza pyramid. The appropriate size for use beneath the head is an overall height small enough to make placing it under the cushion of the head a comfortable thing.

The only incorrect substances would be the baser (copper, zinc, nickel, tin, lead, aluminum) metals. There are better materials which are, in our system of barter, quite dear. (Bartering is an exchange of goods and services between two or more parties without the use of money). These materials are not much better than the substances Ra mentioned before.

Ra mentioned the problems with the action in the King's Chamber of the Giza-type pyramid. So, the channeling group didn't use the King's Chamber radiations but only the third spiral from the top to construct a small pyramid. For energy through the apex angle the Giza pyramid offers an excellent model. Ra told the group to be sure the pyramid is so small that there is no entity small enough to crawl inside it.

The properties of this third spiral energy are such as to move within the field of the physical complex and irradiate (expose to radiation) each cell of the space/time (physical) body and, as this is done, irradiate also the time/space (metaphysical) equivalent which is close aligned with the space/time yellow-ray body. This is not a function of the etheric body or of free will. This is a radiation much like our sun's rays. Thus, it should be used with care.

In most cases, no more than one 30 minute or less application during a diurnal (day) time period would be appropriate. In a few cases, especially where energy will be used for spiritual work, experimentation with two shorter periods might be possible, but any feelings of sudden weariness would be a sign of over-radiation.

There is no application for direct healing using this energy, although, if used in conjunction with meditation, it may offer to a certain percentage of entities some aid in meditation. In most cases it is most helpful in alleviating weariness and in the stimulation of physical or sexual activity.

In transition from a negative third density planet to fourth density the harvest is one of intense disharmony and the planet will express it through distortions such as disease and so forth.

(If anyone thinks Earth is bad, fourth density negative seems much worse as they are servants to the fifth-density negative entities, as it can be related to what is known as Hell and fourth density positive seems much better, as that can be related to what is known as Heaven. Though the Law of One doesn't blink towards the negative or positive path, each is allowed to be pursued. Though, the positive path is easier due to the harmony of all. In sixth density, the negative path would have to jump to the positive side in order to continue in evolution.)

The vibrations from third to fourth negative oriented planet change precisely as they do upon a positively oriented planet. With fourth-density negative comes many abilities and possibilities of which you are familiar. The fourth density is more dense, and it is far more difficult to hide the true vibrations of the mind/body/spirit complex. This enables fourth-density negatives, as well as positives, the chance to form social memory complexes. It enables negatively oriented entities the opportunity for a different set of parameters that shows their power over others and to be service to the self. The conditions are the same as far as the vibrations are concerned.

Each planetary experience is unique. The problems of bellicose (warlike) actions are more likely to be of pressing concern to late third-density negative entities than the Earth's reactions to negativity of the planetary mind, for it is often by such warlike attitudes on a global scale that the necessary negative polarization is achieved.

91

As fourth density occurs, there is a new planet and new physical vehicle system gradually expressing itself, and the parameters of bellicose actions become those of thought rather than manifested weapons.

Physical complex distortions, such as disease and illness, are likely to be found less as fourth-density negative begins to be a probable choice for harvest due to the extreme interest in the self which characterizes the harvestable third-density negative entity. Much more care is taken of the body, as well as much more discipline being offered of the self mentally. This is an orientation of great self-interest and self-discipline. There are still instances of disease which are associated with the mind complex distortions of negative emotions such as anger. However, in a harvestable entity these emotional distortions are much more likely to be used as catalyst in an expressive and destructive sense in regards to anger.

Distortions of mind or body are found in beings which need experiences to aid in polarization. These polarizations may be those entities who have already chosen the path to be followed.

It is more likely for positively oriented individuals to be experiencing body distortions due to the lack of consuming interest in the self and the emphasis on service to others. Moreover, in an unpolarized entity, catalyst of the physical distortion will be generated at random. The hopeful result is the original choice of polarity. Oftentimes this choice is not made but the catalyst continues to be generated. In the negatively oriented individual, the physical body is likely to be more carefully tended and the mind disciplined against physical distortion.

There seems to be many diseases and bodily malfunctions in general on this third density planet. If the mind doesn't use the catalyst offered to the entity, it will then filter through to the body complex and manifest as some form of physical distortion. The more efficient the use of catalyst, the less physical distortion to be found.

Wanderers not only have a congenital difficulty (which is present at birth) in dealing with the third-density vibratory patterns but also a recollection (remembering), that these distortions are not necessary or usual in the home vibration.

Ra overgeneralizes as always, for there are many cases of pre-incarnative decisions which result in physical or mental limitations and distortions. Indeed, on some third-density planetary spheres, catalyst has been used more efficiently. In the case of earth, there is much more inefficient use of catalyst and, therefore, much physical distortion."

Session 67: 8-15-1981

The negative entity (demon) has been observing the instrument's service to the Creator during these sessions and now has a constant level of psychic attack upon the instrument as long as she continues in this service.

Ra: "Variations towards the distortion of intensity of attack occur due to the opportunities presented by the entity in any weakness. At this particular nexus the entity has been dealing with the distortion of pain for some time and this has a cumulatively (increasingly) weakening effect upon physical energy levels. This creates a particularly favorable target of opportunity, and the negative entity has taken this opportunity to attempt to be of service in its own way. It is fortunate for the ongoing vitality of this contact that the instrument is a strong-willed entity with little tendency towards the distortion, called among your people's hysteria, since the dizzying effects of this attack have been constant and at times disruptive for several of your diurnal periods.

However, this particular entity is adapting well to the situation without undue distortions towards fear. Thus, the psychic attack is not successful but does have some draining influence upon the instrument."

An expression of a positively polarized and balanced view of negatively polarized actions can debilitate the strength of the negatively polarized entities actions by the questioner viewing the so-called attack as offering its service with respect to its distortion in their polarized condition now so that the group may fully appreciate its polarity, and they are appreciative and thank the entity for its attempt to serve our One Creator in bringing us knowledge in a more complete sense.

The questioner, Don Elkins, views the psychic attack as an offering of service, therefore Don uses the term psychic greeting instead. This particular negative entity is of the Orion Confederation of fifth density negative, and by time/space light or fifth-density body is used while the space/time fifth-density body remains in fifth density. The consciousness is projected to where the instrument is and is one of the seven bodies that make up its mind/body/spirit complex.

This conscious vehicle attached to the space/time fifth-density physical complex is the vehicle that works in this particular service. This is a trans dimensional nature, not only of space/time to time/space but from density to density.

The efforts of this negative entity attacking the instrument are put forward only reluctantly.

Ra: "The usual attempts upon positively oriented entities or groups of entities are made by minions of the fifth-density Orion leader; these are fourth density. The normal gambit of such fourth-density attack is the tempting of the entity or group of entities away from total polarization towards service to others and toward the aggrandizement of self (making yourself more important or powerful than they really are) or of social organization with which the self identifies. In the case of this particular group, each was given a full range of temptations to cease being of service to each other and to the one Infinite Creator. Each entity declined these choices and instead continued with no significant deviation from the desire for a purely other self-service

94

orientation. At this point one of the fifth-density entities overseeing such detuning processes determined that it would be necessary to terminate the group by magical means, as you understand ritual magic. We have previously discussed the potential for the removal of one of this group by such attack and have noted that by far the most vulnerable is the instrument due to its pre-incarnative physical complex distortions."

The negative entity desires are to misplace one or more of this group in a negative orientation so that it may choose to be of service along the path of service to self. The objective which must precede this is the termination of the physical body viability of one of the group members while the mind/body/spirit complex is within controllable configuration. In Ra's limited understanding their belief is that sending this entity love and light, which each of the group is doing, is the most helpful catalyst which the group may offer this entity. The 5th density negative entity has been as neutralized as possible in Ra's estimation by the groups love offering, and thus its continued presence is perhaps the understandable limit for each polarity of the various views of service each may render (give) to the other.

We have no ability not to serve the Creator since all is the Creator. The frequency someone resonates at determines your choice of service to the One Creator.

Ra: "As it happens, this groups' vibratory patterns and those of Ra are compatible and enable us to speak through this instrument with your support. This is a function of free will.

A portion, seemingly of the Creator, rejoices at your choice to question us regarding the evolution of spirit. A seemingly separate portion would wish for multitudinous (a vast) answer to a great range of queries of a specific nature. Another seemingly separate group of your peoples would wish this correspondence through this instrument to cease, feeling it to be of a negative nature. Upon the many other planes of existence, there are those whose every fiber rejoices at your service, and those such as the

95

entity of whom you have been speaking (the negative entity) which wish only to terminate the life upon the third-density plane of this instrument. All are the Creator. There is one vast panoply (impressive collection of things) of biases and distortions, colors and hues, in an unending pattern. In the case of those with whom you, as entities and as a group, are not in resonance, you wish them love, light, peace, joy and bid them well. No more than this can you do for your portion of the Creator is as it is, and your experience and offering of experience, to be valuable, needs be more and more a perfect representation of who you truly are. Could you, then, serve a negative entity by offering the instrument's life? It is unlikely that you would if this is a true service. Thus, you may see in many cases the loving balance being achieved, the love being offered, light being sent, and the service of the service-to-self-oriented entity gratefully acknowledged while being rejected as not being useful in your journey at this time. Thus, you serve One Creator without paradox."

The instrument at a young age had many eye infections that caused great difficulties at a young age. The scars of these distortions remained and the sinus system remains distorted. Thus, the negative entity works with these distortions to produce a loss of balance (the dizzying effect) and a slight lack of ability to use the optic apparatus. (The optic apparatus is a complex system of nerves and other structures that transmits visual information from the eyes to the brain.)

Ra: "This entity is able to penetrate in time/space configuration the field of this particular entity. It has moved through the quarantine without any vehicle and thus has been more able to escape detection by the net of the Guardians.

This is the great virtue of the magical working whereby consciousness is sent forth essentially without vehicle as light. The light would work instantly upon an untuned individual by suggestion; that is, the stepping out in front of the traffic because the suggestion is that there is no traffic. This entity, as each in this group, is enough disciplined in the ways of love and light that it is not suggestible to any great extent. However, there is a predisposition of the physical complex which this entity is making maximal use of as regards to the instrument, hoping, for instance, by means of increasing dizziness to cause the instrument to fall or to indeed walk in front of your traffic because of impaired vision.

The magical principles may be loosely translated into your system of magic, whereby symbols are used and traced and visualized in order to develop the power of the light."

The fifth-density entity visualizes certain symbols. These symbols are of a nature where their continued use would have some power or charge. In fifth density, light is as visible a tool as our pencil's writing. The entity configures a light used to create sufficient purity of environment for the entity to place its consciousness in a carefully created light vehicle which then uses the tools of light to do its working. The will and presence are those of the entity doing the working.

The fifth-density entity penetrated the quarantine through a very slight window which less magically oriented entities or groups could not have used to their advantage. This window exists because of free will. This is a portion of the random effect, and the group experiences the same type of balancing in receiving the psychic attacks as the planet in general receives because of the window effect. As the planetary sphere accepts more highly evolved positive entities or groups with information to offer, the same opportunity must be offered to similarly wise negatively oriented entities or groups.

Ra's view expresses appreciation of this opportunity. This is an intensive opportunity in that it is quite marked in its effects, both actual and potential, and as it affects the instrument's distortions towards pain and other difficulties such as dizziness, it enables the instrument to continuously choose to serve others and serve the Creator.

Similarly, it offers a continual opportunity for each in the group to express support under more distorted or difficult circumstances of the other-self experiencing the brunt of this attack, thus being able to demonstrate the love and light of the Infinite Creator and, furthermore, choosing working by working to continue to serve as messengers for this information which Ra attempts to offer and to serve the Creator thereby.

Thus, the opportunities are quite noticeable, as well as the distortions caused by this circumstance.

This attack is offered to all in the group.

Ra: "The questioner has been offered the service of doubting the self and of becoming disheartened over various distortions of the personal nature. This entity has not chosen to use these opportunities, and the Orion entity has basically ceased to be interested in maintaining constant surveillance of this entity.

The scribe is under constant surveillance and has been offered numerous opportunities for the intensification of the mental/emotional distortions and in some cases the connection matrices between mental/emotional complexes and the physical complex counterpart. As this entity has become aware of these attacks, it has become much less pervious (passable) to them. This is the particular cause of the great intensification and constancy of the surveillance of the instrument, for it is the weak link due to factors beyond its control within this incarnation."

Ra finds great humor in Don Elkins attempt to be of polarized service to the opposite polarity. Since Don wanted to confirm that there was nothing that they could do for the fifth density entity besides offer love and light for the negative entity. There is a natural difficulty in wanting to offer service to the opposite polarity, since what Don considers service is considered nonservice by the negative entity. As you send this entity love and light and wish it well, it loses its polarity and needs to regroup.

Thus, it would not consider Don's service as such. On the other hand, if Don allowed it to be of service by removing this instrument from that midst, Don might perceive this as not being of service. Don has a balanced and polarized view of the Creator; two services offered, mutually rejected, and in a state of equilibrium in which free will is preserved and each allowed to go upon its own path of experiencing the One Infinite Creator. There's unification in sixth density of these two paths.

In working with the mind, we are working with one complex and have not yet attempted to penetrate intelligent infinity. Archetypes are portions of the One Infinite Creator or aspects of its face. Archetypes do not give the same yield of these complexes to any two seekers. Each seeker will experience each archetype in the characteristics within the complex of the archetype most important to it. An example of this is the questioner viewing the fool archetype as The Prodigal Son corresponding to every entity who seems to have strayed from unity and seeks to return to the One Infinite Creator. One great aspect of the fool is the aspect of faith, the walking into space without regard for what is to come next. This is, of course, foolish but is part of the characteristic of the spiritual neophyte (beginner).

Session 68: 8-18-1981

Ra instructed the instrument to refrain from calling Ra unless it is within this set of circumscribed circumstances, such as these channeling sessions with the group and Ra. The instrument was slipping into trance state during one of the normal Sunday night meditations, where she was asked a question about the Ra Material from Ra's brothers and sisters of the wisdom density known as Latwii.

Ra: "This instrument thought to itself, "I do not know this answer. I wish I were channeling Ra." The ones of Latwii found themselves in the position of being approached by the Orion entity which seeks to be of service in its own way. The instrument began to prepare for Ra contact. Latwii knew that if this was completed,

99

the Orion entity would have an opportunity which Latwii wished to avoid.

It is fortunate for this instrument, firstly, that Latwii is of fifth density and able to deal with that particular vibratory complex which the Orion entity was manifesting and, secondly, that there were those in the support group at that time which sent great amounts of support to the instrument in this crux. Thus, what occurred was the ones of Latwii never let go of this instrument, although this came perilously close to breaking the Way of Confusion. It continued to hold its connection with the mind/body/spirit complex of the instrument and to generate information through it even as the instrument began to slip out of its physical vehicle.

The act of continued communication caused the entity to be unable to grasp the instrument's mind/body/spirit complex, and after but a small measure of your space/time, Latwii recovered the now completely amalgamated (formed a close union without complete loss of individual identities of the) instrument and gave it continued communication to steady it during the transition back into integration."

The plan of the fifth-density negative entity was to take the mind/body/spirit complex while it was separated from its yellow-body physical complex shell, to then place this mind/body/spirit complex within the negative portions of your time/space. The shell would then become that of the unknowing, unconscious entity and could be worked upon to cause malfunction which could end in a coma and then in death of the body. At this point the Higher Self of the instrument would have the choice of leaving the mind/body/spirit complex in negative time/space (non-physical reality) or of allowing incarnation in space/time (physical reality) of equivalent vibration and polarity distortions. Thus, this entity would become a negatively polarized entity without the advantage of native negative polarization. It would find a long path to the Creator under these circumstances, although the path would inevitably end well.

The Higher Self could allow the mind/body/spirit complex to remain in time/space (metaphysical/another dimension). However, it is unlikely that the Higher Self would do so indefinitely, due to its distortion towards the belief that the function of the mind/body/spirit complex is to experience and learn from other selves, thus experiencing the Creator. A highly polarized positive mind/body/spirit complex surrounded by negative portions of space/time will experience only darkness, for like the magnet, there is no likeness. Thus, a barrier is automatically formed. This darkness is experienced in Negative time/space.

If this happened to a Wanderer of sixth density and went into negative time/space, it would be sixth-density negative time/space and would incarnate into sixth-density negative space/time.

The strength of the polarization would be matched as far as possible. In some positive sixth-density Wanderers, the approximation would not quite be complete due to the paucity (scarcity) of negative sixth-density energy fields of the equivalent strength. In the case of this instrument, this could happen because the Wanderer extracted in the trance state, leaving the third-density physical, does not have the full capability to magically defend itself. This is also correct when applied almost without exception to those instruments working in trance which haven't experienced magical training in time/space trans-dimensionally in the present incarnation. The entities of our density capable of magical defense in this situation are extremely rare.

The entity seeking magical ability for defense against negative entities must do so in a certain manner. Ra's general instructions is to never call upon Ra in any way while unprotected by the configuration which is at this time, present. (There's protection in the channeling process by a group being there instead of alone in meditation.)

To take an entity before it is ready and offer it the scepter (an ornamented staff) of magical power (carried by rulers as a symbol of sovereignty) is to infringe in an unbalanced manner.

The fifth-density negative entity is alerted that this channeling group exists and becomes aware of power.

Ra: "I am Ra. The entity becomes aware of power. This power has the capacity of energizing those which may be available for harvest. This entity is desirous of disabling this power source. It sends its legions. Temptations are offered. They are ignored or rejected. The power source persists and indeed improves its inner connections of harmony and love of service.

The entity determines that it must needs attempt the disabling itself. By means of projection it enters the vicinity of this power source. It assesses the situation. It is bound by the first distortion but may take advantage of any free-will distortion. The free-will, pre-incarnative distortions of the instrument with regard to the physical vehicle seem the most promising target. Any distortion away from service to others is also appropriate.

When the instrument leaves its physical vehicle, it does so freely. Thus, the misplacement of the mind/body/spirit complex of the instrument would not be a violation of its free will if it followed the entity freely. This is the process. We are aware of your pressing desire to know how to become impervious (unaffected) as a group to any influences such as this. The processes which you seek are a matter of your free choice. You are aware of the principles of magical work. We cannot speak to advise but can only suggest, as we have before, that it would be appropriate for this group to embark upon such a path as a group, but not individually, for obvious reason."

The positive polarity sees love in all things and that's why one might follow a negative entity to negative time/space (non-physical/another dimension). The negative polarity is clever and able to misplace a mind/body/spirit complex through the positive entities free will. If the negative polarity used any other approach that did not use the free will of the other self, he would lose polarization and magical power.

Session 69: 8-29-1981

Ra suggested for future working the combing of this antenna-like material (hair) into a more orderly configuration prior to the working.

Ra: "The mind/body/spirit complex which freely leaves the third-density physical complex is vulnerable when the appropriate protection is not at hand. You may perceive carefully that very few entities which choose to leave their physical complexes are doing work of such a nature as to attract the polarized attention of negatively oriented entities. The danger to most in trance state, is the touching of the physical complex (body) in such a manner as to attract the mind/body/spirit complex back thereunto or to damage the means by which that which you call ectoplasm is being recalled."

Ectoplasm, in spirituality is a mysterious, usually light-colored, substance that is said to exude from the body of spiritualist medium in trance and may then take the shape of a face, a hand, or a complete body.

Ra: "This instrument is an anomaly in that it is well that the instrument not be touched or artificial light thrown upon it while in the trance state. However, the ectoplasmic activity is interiorized. The main difficulty is then the previously discussed negative removal of the entity under its free will.

That this can happen only in the trance state is not completely certain, but it is highly probable that in another out-of-body experience such as death, the entity here examined would, as most positively polarized entities, have a great deal of protection from comrades, guides, and portions of the self which would be aware of the transfer of physical death."

Protective positive guides or angelic presences would be available in every condition except for the trance state, which is anomalistic (uncommon) with respect to the others.

The uniqueness of this trance state with Ra is the intent to serve others with the highest attempt at near purity which Ra and the group as comrades may achieve.

Ra: "This has alerted a much more determined friend of negative polarity which is interested in removing this particular opportunity.

We may say once again two notes: Firstly, we searched long to find an appropriate channel or instrument and an appropriate support group. If this opportunity is ended, we shall be grateful for that which has been done, but the possibility/probability vortices indicating the location of this configuration again are slight. Secondly, we thank you for we know what you sacrifice in order to do that which you as a group wish to do.

We will not deplete this instrument insofar as we are able. We have attempted to speak of how the instrument may deplete itself through too great a dedication to the working. All these things and all else we have said has been heard. We are thankful. In the present situation we express thanks to the entities who call themselves Latwii."

All deaths, whether by natural means, accident or suicide, the negative friends are not able to remove an entity. This is largely because the entity without the attachment to the space/time physical complex is far more aware and without the gullibility which is somewhat the hallmark of those who love wholeheartedly.

However, the death, if natural, would undoubtedly be the more harmonious; the death by murder being confused and the entity needing some time/space (time in another

104

dimension/afterlife) to get its bearings, the death by suicide causing the necessity for much healing work and reincarnating into third density for the renewed opportunity of learning the lessons set by the Higher Self."

If the entity is not trying to be of service and passes away from accident, medical anesthetic or drugs, the negative entities would not find it possible to remove the mind/body/spirit complex.

The dangerous characteristic is the willing of the entity outward from the physical body of third density for the purpose of service-to-others. In any other situation this circumstance would not be in effect. The free will of the instrument is indeed a necessary part of the opportunity afforded the Orion group. However, this free will applies only to the instrument. The entire hope of the Orion group is to infringe upon free will without losing polarity. Thus, this group, if represented by a wise entity, attempts to be clever.

A Wanderer has been so infringed upon in the past by a negative adept and was placed in negative time/space. The path back to the conscious state after trance firstly revolves about the Higher Self's reluctance to enter negative space/time (incarnation). This may be a significant part of the length of that path. Secondly, when a positively oriented entity incarnates in a thoroughly negative environment, it must need to learn/teach the lessons of the love of self, thus becoming one with its other selves.

When this has been accomplished, the entity may then choose to release the potential difference and change polarities. However, the process of learning the accumulated lessons of love of self may be quite lengthy. Also, the entity, in learning these lessons, may lose much positive orientation during the process, and the choice of reversing polarities may be delayed until the mid-sixth density. All of this is time consuming, although the end result is well.

There has only been one Wanderer that came to Earth that has experienced this displacement during this master cycle into negative time/space (in another dimension).

The incarnative process involves being incarnated from time/space (metaphysical) to space/time (physical), so the Higher Self is reluctant to enter negative space/time (physical incarnation).

When first moved into negative time/space, the positive entity experiences nothing but darkness. Then, by incarnation into negative space/time by the Higher Self, it experiences a negative space/time environment with negatively polarized other selves. The positively oriented individual makes a poor student of the love of self and thus spends much more time than those native to that pattern of vibrations. The misplacement is a function of his free will.

Firstly, A positively oriented entity moving into negative time/space is like receiving a poorly marked map and is quite incorrect. It sets out wishing only to reach the point of destination, but becomes confused by the faculty authority and not knowing the territory through which it drives, becomes hopelessly lost.

Free will may at times encounter circumstances when calculations will be awry. This is so in all aspects of the life experience. Although there are no mistakes, there are no surprises.

Secondly, there's a magical charge or metaphysical power when the group does these channelings with Ra. Those who do work of power are available for communication to and from entities of roughly similar power. It is fortunate that the Orion entity does not have the native power of this group. However, it is quite disciplined, whereas this group lacks the finesse equivalent to its power. Each is working in consciousness, but the group has not begun a work as a group. The individual work is helpful, for the group is mutually an aid, to one another.

In order for the instrument not to go into trance other than at a protected channeling such as the group does with Ra:

1- The instrument must improve the disciplined subconscious taboo against requesting Ra, except in the protected group channeling. This would involve daily conscious and serious thought.

2- The second safeguard is the refraining from the opening of this instrument to questions and answers for the present.

3- The hand may be held to keep the instrument in its physical complex during meditation. Also, in the event that, unlikely as it may seem, the entity grew able to leave the physical body, the auric infringement and tactile pressure would cause the mind/body/spirit complex to refrain from leaving. Long practice of the art which intuits here would be helpful. Ra cannot speak of methodology, for the infringement would be most great. However, group effort may do.

Although Ra cannot speak with precision of the techniques and ways of practicing white magical arts or if rituals are designed or not by a particular group for their own particular use or if they are just as good or possibly better than these practiced by the order of the Golden Dawn and other magical groups. Ra notes some gratification that the questioner has penetrated some of the gist of a formidable (intimidating) system of service and discipline.

Session 70: 9-9-1981

The instrument complained of intensive psychic attack for the past day. Ra said the cause is the intensive seeking of enlightenment. The seeking through asking Ra questions during channelings has intensified the attack. Thus, the Orion visitor strives with more and more intensity to disturb the instruments vital energy as this group intensifies its dedication to service through enlightenment.

There is an infinite range of possibility of service/disservice in time-regression hypnosis, an aiding in memory. It has nothing to do with the hypnotist. It has only to do with the hypnotized entity makes of the information gained if the hypnotist desires to serve and if such a service is performed only upon sincere request, the hypnotist is attempting to be of service.

The Higher Self is reluctant to allow its mind/body/spirit to enter negative time/space, since it would be like a prison to us.

The Higher Self is the entity of mid-sixth density, which, turning back, offers this service to its self.

We are all existing at all levels (densities) simultaneously. Your Higher Self is you in mid-sixth density and your Higher Self is yourself in your future. All mind/body/spirit complexes that exist below mid-sixth density has a Higher Self at the level of mid-sixth density.

The Higher Self protects when possible and guides when asked, but the force of free will is paramount. The seeming determinism and free will melt when it is accepted that there is such a thing as true simultaneity. The Higher Self is the end result of all the development experienced by the mind/body/spirit complex to that point.

In time/space, which is precisely as much of yourself as is space/time, all times are simultaneous just as, in your geography, your cities and villages are all functioning's, hustling, and alive with entities going about their business at once. So, it is in time/space with the self.

A positive entity displaced to negative time/space (not incarnate) has the Higher Self being reluctant to this. Each time/space is an analog (an interior analog of the external world) of a particular sort of vibration of space/time. When a negative time/space is entered by an entity, the next experience will be that of the appropriate space/time (going into that next incarnation).

108

This is normally done by the form-making body (indigo body) of a mind/body/spirit complex which places the entity in the proper time/space incarnation.

If a Wanderer of fourth, fifth, or sixth density dies from this third-density state, the time/space density will depend upon the approval by the council of Nine. Some Wanderers offer themselves for one incarnation, while others offer themselves for varying lengths up to and including the last two cycles of 25,000 years for each cycle. If the agreed upon mission is complete, the Wanderer's mind/body/spirit complex will go to the home vibration.

There have been a few Wanderers on this planet for the 50,000 years now. There have been many more which chose to join this last cycle of 25,000 years, and many, many more which have come for harvest.

The position in negative time/space is pre-incarnative. After death of the physical complex in yellow-ray activation, the mind/body/spirit complex moves to a far different portion of time/space in which the indigo body will allow much healing and review to take place before any movement is made towards another incarnative experience.

A miscalculation would be the perception of time/space being no more homogeneous (alike) than space/time. It is as complex and complete a system of illusions, dances, and patterns as is space/time, and has structured a system of natural laws.

George Adamski photographed the bell-shaped craft when Ra came to Earth 18,000 and 11,000 years ago. These craft looked somewhat like a bell; they had portholes around them in the upper portions, and had three hemispheres at 120 degrees apart underneath. A construct of thought constructed them in time/space. This portion of time/space approaches the speed of light. In time/space, the conditions are such that time becomes infinite and mass ceases, so that one which is able to skim the boundary strength of this time/space is able to become placed where it will.

When Ra was where they wished to be, they then clothed the construct of light that appeared as a crystal bell. This was formed through the boundary into space/time. Thus, there were two constructs: time/space or immaterial construct, and the space/time. (Therefore, if the second word is time, then it's in physical reality with time. If the second word is space, then it's in metaphysical reality in space without time).

The particular shape and three hemispheres at the bottom seemed aesthetically pleasing form to Ra and one well suited to those limited uses which Ra must needs make of our space/time motivating requirements.

The three hemispheres at the bottom were aesthetic and part of a propulsion system. They were not landing gear.

Space/time is physics.

Time/space is metaphysics. These concepts are mechanical, they are not central to the spiritual evolution of the mind/body/spirit complex. The study of love and light is far more productive in its motion towards unity in those entities pondering (carefully thinking before reaching a conclusion on) such concepts.

The entity that incarnated into negative space/time (incarnation) will not find it possible to maintain any significant positive polarity, as negativity, when pure, is a type of gravity well, pulling all into it. Thus, the entity while remembering its learned and preferred polarity, must make use of the catalyst given and recapitulate (briefly summarize) the lessons of service to self in order to build up enough polarity in order to cause the potential to occur for reversal.

Ra is attempting to be of the greatest aid to the group by taking care not to deplete this instrument, so Ra would ask if there were any more questions before ending the session to let the instrument keep her reserved energy and Ra was glad to speak with the group. The instrument had arranged its subconscious to accept this channeling session.

Session 71: 9-18-1981

The connection between polarization and harvestability is most important in third-density harvest. In this density an increase in the serving of others or the serving of self will almost inevitably increase the ability of an entity to enjoy a higher intensity of light. Thus, in this density, it is hardly possible to polarize without increasing in harvestability.

In fifth-density harvest, polarization has very little to do with harvestability.

The unmanifested being does its work without aid from other selves. There's an inevitable connection between the unmanifested self and the metaphysical time/space analog (equivalent) of the space/time self. The activities of meditation, contemplation and the internal balancing of thoughts and reactions are those activities of the unmanifested-self more closely aligned with the metaphysical self.

Ra: "The hallmark of time/space is the inequity between time and space. In your space/time the spatial (structural) orientation of material causes a tangible framework for illusion. In time/space the inequity is upon the shoulders of that property known to you as time. This property renders (gives) entities and experiences intangible in a relative sense. In your framework, each particle or core vibration moves at a velocity which approaches the speed of light from the direction of supraliminal velocities. (Supraliminal velocities are speeds exceeding the speed of light).

Thus, the time/space or metaphysical experience is that which is very finely tuned and, although an analog of space/time, lacking in its tangible characteristics. In these metaphysical planes there is a great deal of time which is used to review and re-review the biases and learn/teachings of a prior space/time incarnation.

The extreme fluidity of these regions makes it possible for much to be penetrated which must be absorbed before the process of healing of an entity may be accomplished. Each entity is located in a somewhat immobile state, much as you are located in space/time in a somewhat immobile state in time. In this immobile space the entity has been placed by the form maker and Higher Self so that it may be in the proper configuration for learn/teaching that which it has received in the space/time incarnation.

Depending upon this time/space locus, there will be certain helpers which assist in this healing process. The process involves seeing in full the experience, seeing it against the backdrop of the mind/body/spirit complex total experience, forgiving the self for all missteps as regards the missed guideposts during the incarnation, and, finally, the careful assessment of the next necessities for learning. This is done entirely by the Higher Self until an entity has become conscious in space/time of the process and means of spiritual evolution, at which time the entity will consciously take part in all decisions."

The processes of healing and review for the negative polarization is similar for the positive path as well.

Ra: "I am Ra. The process in space/time of the forgiveness and acceptance is much like that in time/space, in that the qualities of the process are analogous (similar, but different categories). However, while in space/time it is not possible to determine the course of events beyond the incarnation, but only to correct present imbalances. In time/space it is not possible to correct any unbalanced actions but rather to perceive the imbalances and thusly forgive the self for that which is.

112

The decisions then are made to set up the possibility/probabilities of correcting these imbalances in future space/time experiences. The advantage of time/space is that, working in darkness with a tiny candle, one may correct imbalances."

The processes of healing and review occur upon all planets which have given birth to sub-Logoi such as yourselves. The percentage of inhabited planets is approximately 10 percent.

Approximately 32 percent of stars have planets, while 6 percent have some sort of clustering material which upon some densities might be inhabitable. This octave of infinite knowledge of the One Creator is as it is throughout the One Infinite Creation, with variations programmed by sub-Logoi of major galaxies and minor galaxies.

Our sub-Logos such as our sun uses free will to modify only slightly a much more general idea of created evolution, so that the general plan of created evolution seem to be uniform throughout the One Infinite Creation. The process is for the sub-Logoi to grow through the densities and find their way back to the original thought through free will.

Each entity is of a path that leads to one destination. Many roads that travel through many places but eventually merge into one large center, merging back into the Creator at the seventh density harvest.

More applicable would be the thought that each entity contains within it all of the densities and sub-densities of the octave, so that in each entity, no matter what its choices lead it, its great internal blueprint is one with all others. Thusly its experiences will fall into the patterns of the journey back to the original Logos. This is done through free will, but the materials from which choices can be made are one blueprint.

Pure negativity acts as a gravity well, pulling all into it. Positivity has a much weaker effect due to the strong element of recognition of free will in any positivity approaching purity. Thus, although the negatively oriented entity may find it difficult to polarize negatively in the midst of such resounding harmony, it will not find it impossible.

The negative polarization is one which does not accept the concept of the free will of other selves. Thusly, in a social complex whose negativity approaches purity, the pull upon other selves is constant. A positively oriented entity in such a situation would desire for other selves to have their free will and thusly would find itself removed from its ability to exercise its own free will, for the free will of negatively oriented entities is bent upon conquest (control of entities or places).

Magic is the ability to create changes in consciousness at will. This is the burden of the adept. In magic, one is working with one's unmanifested self in body, in mind, and in spirit, the mixture depending upon the nature of the working.

(Manifested self is physical. Unmanifested self would be metaphysical).

These workings are facilitated by the enhancement of the activation of the indigo-ray energy center. The indigo-ray energy center is fed, as are all energy centers, by experience, but for more than other energy centers is fed by the disciplines of the personality.

White magic may be worked for the purpose of altering only the self or the place of working. To aid the self in polarization towards love and light is to aid the planetary vibration. The heart of white magic is the experience of the joy of union with the Creator. This joy will of necessity radiate throughout the life experience of the positive adept. It is for this reason that sexual magic is not restricted solely to the negatively oriented polarizing adepts but, when most carefully used, has its place in high magic as it, when correctly pursued, joins body, mind and spirit with the One Infinite Creator. Union with the One Infinite Creator will result in service to others.

Ra stated in a previous session that they searched for some time to find a group such as this one (Don Elkins, Carla Rueckert and Jim McCarty). This search was for the purpose of communicating the Law of One and to make reparation for distortions of this law set in motion by their naïve actions of our past. (18,000 and 11,000 years ago). Ra does not expect to make full reparations for these distortions. The attempt is far more important to them than the completeness of the result. What is distorted cannot, to Ra's knowledge, be fully undistorted but only illuminated somewhat. Ra conducted this search in time-space, for in this illusion one may quite readily see entities as vibratory complexes and groups as harmonics within vibratory complexes.

The most important aspect of this communication as the group is a vehicle of partial enlightenment for those on Earth now who have become aware of their part in their own evolutionary process. This is the goal of all artifacts and experiences which entities may come in contact with, and is not only the property of Ra or this contact.

Ra said that the instrument should hold back a portion of energy for reserve. This will lengthen the number or workings the group may have. (This is an example of wisdom).

Session 72: 10-14-1981

The banishing ritual that the group performs before a channeling working with Ra purifies the places and the screening of influences that they do not wish to be there, such as negative entities. (The Circle of One.)

What caused the instrument to become in a condition towards unconsciousness in the last two meditations:

Ra: "The entity which greets this instrument from the Orion group first attempted to cause the mind/body/spirit, which you call spirit, to leave the physical complex of yellow ray in the deluded belief that it was preparing for the Ra contact. You are familiar with this tactic and its consequences. The instrument, with no pause, upon feeling this greeting, called for the grounding within the physical complex by requesting that the hand be held. Thus, the greatest aim of the Orion entity was not achieved. However, it discovered that those present were not capable of distinguishing between unconsciousness with the mind/body/spirit intact and the trance state in which the mind/body/spirit complex is not present.

Therefore, it applied to the fullest extent the greeting which causes the dizziness and in meditation without protection caused, in this instrument, simple unconsciousness, as in what you would call fainting or vertigo. The Orion entity consequently used this tactic to stop the Ra contact from having the opportunity to be accomplished."

During the instrument's scheduled hand operation next month, it is extremely improbable that the instrument going under general anesthetic into an unconscious state would allow psychic attacks from Orion entities. This is due to the necessity for the intention of the being, when departing the yellow-ray physical complex, to be serving the Creator in the most specific fashion for a potential attack to occur. The attitude of the individual is of paramount importance for the Orion entity to be able to be effective. During channeling's, the instruments attitude is to serve the Creator so the Orion's attack, during anesthetic, the attitude wouldn't be on serving the Creator, so it would be extremely improbable for a negative entity to attack during the unconscious state of her hand operation.

Ra: "The Law of Confusion or Free will is utterly paramount in the workings of the infinite creation. That which is intended has as much intensity of attraction to the polar opposite as the intensity of the intention or desire.

Thus, those whose desires are shallow or transitory experience only ephemeral (lasts a very short time) configuration of what might be called the magical circumstance. There is a turning point, a fulcrum (the supporting point of a lever/ a pivot) which swings as a mind/body/spirit complex tunes its will to service. If this will and desire is for service to others, the corresponding polarity will be activated. In the circumstance of this group, there are three such wills acting as one with the instrument in the central position of fidelity to service. This is as it must be for the balance of the working and the continuance of the contact. Our vibratory complex is one-pointed in these working also, and our will to service is also of some degree of purity. This has created the attraction of the polar opposite which you experience.

We may note that such a configuration of free will, one-pointed in service to others, also has the potential for the alerting of a great mass of light strength. This positive light strength, however, operates also under free will and must be invoked. We could not speak to this and shall not guide you, for the nature of this contact is such that the purity of your free will must, above all things, be preserved. Thus, you wend your way through experiences, discovering those biases which may be helpful."

Ra: "Firstly, those of negative polarity do not operate with respect to free will unless it is necessary. They call themselves and will infringe whenever they feel it possible.

Secondly, they are limited by the great Law of Confusion in that, for the most part, they are unable to enter this planetary sphere of influence and are able to use the windows of time/space distortion only insofar as there is some calling to balance the positive calling. Once they are here, their desire is conquest (control of others).

Thirdly, in the instance of this instrument's being removed permanently from this space/time, it is necessary to allow the instrument to leave its yellow-ray physical complex of its free will. Thus, trickery has been attempted.

The use of the light forms being generated is such as to cause such entities to discover a wall through which they cannot pass. This is due to the energy complexes of the light beings and aspects of the One Infinite Creator invoked (call upon) and evoked (bring to the conscious mind) in the building of the wall of light."

Everything that the group experiences with the contact, their distortion with knowledge in order to serve, the Orion entity's distortion towards reducing the effectiveness of this contact is all a result of free will in creating the free atmosphere for the Creator to become more knowledgeable of Itself through the interplay of its portions, one with respect to the other.

The instrument has great distortions in the direction of mind complex activity, spirit complex activity, and that great conduit to the Creator, the will. Therefore, this instrument's vital energy, even in the absence of any physical reserve measurable, is quite substantial. Physical activities are a far greater distortion in lessening of the vital energy than if used in her deepest desires of serving the Creator. The overuse of this vital energy is, to be literal, the rapid removal of life force.

The proper ritual of this group could use the large amount of light available for recharging the vital energy of the instrument. However, Ra cautions against any working that raises up any personality and realize all are One. Rather it is well to be fastidious in the working." (Fastidious means very attentive to accuracy and details).

The group included "Shin" in the banishing ritual, "Yod-Heh-Vau-Heh" to make it "Yod-Heh-Shin-Vau-Heh." This is helpful especially to the instrument whose distortions vibrate greatly in congruency with this sound vibration complex.

118

The group will now have group meditations for protection for the instrument. Purifying the place of working with the Banishing ritual daily would be most effective for the group in protection against psychic attacks and negative entities.

The opportunity for the Orion entity is completely dependent upon the instrument's condition of awareness and readiness. Ra would suggest that this instrument is still too much the neophyte (new to the subject or belief) to open its self to questions since that is the format used by Ra. As the instrument grows in awareness this precaution may become unnecessary.

Why there isn't protection at the floor or bottom of the banishing ritual:

Ra: "The development of the psychic greeting is possible only through the energy centers, starting from a station which you might call within the violet ray moving through the adept's energy center and therefrom towards the target of opportunity. Depending upon the vibratory nature and purpose of greeting, be it positive or negative, the entity will be energized or blocked in the desired way.

We of Ra approach this instrument in narrow-band contact through violate ray. Others might pierce down through this ray to any energy center. We, for instance, make great use of this instrument's blue-ray energy center as we are attempting to communicate our distortion/understanding of *The Law of One*.

The entity of Orion pierces the same violet ray and moves to two places to attempt most of its nonphysical opportunities. It activates the green-ray energy center while further blocking indigo-ray energy center. This combination causes confusion in the instrument and subsequent over-activity in unwise proportions in physical complex workings. It simply seeks out the distortions pre-incarnatively programmed and developed in incarnative state.

119

The energies of life itself, being the One Infinite Creator, flow from the south pole of the body seen in its magnetic form. Thus, only the Creator may, through the feet, enter the energy shell of the body to any effect. The effects of the adept are those from the upper direction, and thus the building of the wall of light is quite propitious. (favorable, a good chance of success)"

SESSION 73: 10-21-1981

The banishing ritual of the group has gained with each working in making efficacious (a successful desired result of) the purity of contact needed not only for the Ra contact but for any working of the adept.

Don Elkins thanks Ra for the opportunity to be of service to those on Earth who want the information that the group gains during the Ra contact.

One-pointed in service to others has the potential of alerting a great mass of light strength. In invocation (calling on for assistance) and evocation (calling forth) of negative entities or qualities, the expression alerts the positively oriented equivalent. However, those upon the service to others path wait to be called and can only send love.

Those upon the positive path may call upon the light strength in direct proportion to the strength and purity of their will to serve. Those upon the negative path may call upon the dark strength in direct proportion to the strength and purity of their will to serve.

The great way of the development of the light in the microcosmic mind/body/spirit is assumed that the adept will have its energy centers functioning smoothly and in a balanced manner to its best effort before a magical working. All magical workings are based upon evocation and/or invocation.

120

The first invocation of any magical working is that invocation of the magical personality. In the working of the adept alerting the light strength the first station is the beginning of the invocation of this magical personality, which is invoked by the motion of putting on something. If you do not have an item of apparel or talisman, the gesture of visualization is appropriate.

The second station is the evocation of the great cross of life. This is an extension of the magical personality to become the Creator. All invocations and evocations are drawn through the violet energy center. This may then be construed through whatever energy centers are desired to be used.

The action of the upward-spiraling light that enters through the feet is drawn by the will to meet the inner light of the One Infinite Creator may be likened to the beating of the heart and the movement of the muscles surrounding the lungs and all the other functions of the parasympathetic nervous system. The calling of the adept is like the nerve and muscle actions and over which the mind/body/spirit complex has conscious control.

Where the two directions meet of the upward-spiraling light and the light invoked through the crown chakra, is the measure of the development of the particular entity.

Ra: "Each visualization, regardless of the point of the working, begins with some work within the indigo ray. As you may be aware, the ritual which you have begun is completely working within the indigo ray. This is well for it is the gateway. From this beginning, light may be invoked for communication or for healing.

You may note that in the ritual which we offered you to properly begin the Ra workings, the first focus is upon the Creator. We would further note a point which is both subtle and of some interest. The upward-spiraling light developed in its path by the will and, ultimately reaching a high place of mating with the inward fire of the One Creator, still is only preparation for the work upon the mind/body/spirit which may be done by the adept. There is some crystallization of the energy centers used during each working, so that the magician becomes more and more that which it seeks.

More importantly, the time/space (metaphysical) mind/body/spirit analog, which is evoked as the magical personality, has its only opportunity to gain rapidly from the experience of the catalytic action available to the third-density space/time mind/body/spirit totality of an entity."

In the magical personality, desire, will, and polarity are the key factors in this process.

In examining the polarity of a service-to-others working, the free will must be seen as paramount. (Paramount means more important than anything else, supreme.) Many so-called evangelists which we have in our society are attempting to generate positive changes in consciousness while abridging free will. This causes the blockage of the magical nature of the working except in those cases wherein an entity freely desires to accept the working of the evangelist.

Jesus of Nazareth offered itself as teacher to those mind/body/spirit complexes which gathered to hear and even then, spoke as through a veil so as to leave room for those not wishing to hear. When this entity was asked to heal, it often times did so, always sending the working with two admonitions: Firstly, that the entity healed had been healed by its faith-that is, its ability to allow and accept changes through the violet ray into the gateway of intelligent energy; secondly, saying always, "tell no one." These are the working which attempt to maximize quality of free will while maintaining fidelity to the positive purity of the working.

Ra are humble messengers of *The Law of One*. To them there are no paradoxes. Jesus' healings seem magical and, therefore, seem to infringe on free will but do not, for the distortions of perceptions are as many as witnesses, and each

122

witness sees what it desires to see. Infringement of free will occurs in this circumstance of healing only if the entity doing the working takes credit for this event or its own skills. He who states that no working comes from it but only through it is not infringing on free will.

Jesus accumulated twelve disciples to have those that will learn from him and then teach. Those drawn to this entity were accepted by him without regard for any outcome. This entity accepted the honor/duty placed upon it by its nature and its sense that to speak was its mission.

In the exercise of the fire, the healer would be working with the same energy as entering through the crown chakra.

Ra: "When the magical personality has been seated in the green-ray center for healing work, the energy may be seen to be the crystalline center through which body energy is channeled. This particular form of healing uses both the energy of the adept and the energy of the upward-spiraling light. As the green-ray center becomes more brilliant, and we would note this brilliance does not imply over-activation but rather crystallization, the energy of the green-ray center of the body complex spirals twice; firstly, clockwise from the green-ray energy center to the right shoulder, through the head, the right elbow, down through the solar plexus, and to the left hand. This sweeps all the body complex energy into a channel which then rotates the great circle clockwise again from the left to the feet, to the right hand, to the crown, to the left hand, and so forth.

Thus, the incoming body energy, crystallized, regularized, and channeled by the adept's personality reaching to the green-ray energy center, may then pour out the combined energies of the adept which is incarnate, thus offering the service of healing to an entity requesting that service. This basic situation is accomplished as well when there is an entity which is working through a channel to heal."

The transfer of light, would affect the patient to be healed in polarization. The entity may or may not accept any percentage of this polarized life energy which is being offered. In the occasion of the laying on of hands, this energy is more specifically channeled and the opportunity for acceptance of this energy similarly more specific.

It may be seen that the King's Chamber effect is not attempted in this form of working but rather the addition to one, whose energies are low, of the opportunity for the budding up of those energies. Many illnesses can be aided by such means.

There are various forms of healing. In many, only the energy of the adept is used when their energy centers are suitably configured and is then able to channel light, through its properly configured energy centers to the one to be healed.

If the one wishing to be healed, though sincere, remains unhealed, you may consider pre-incarnative choices. The more helpful aid to this unhealed entity may be the suggestion that it meditate upon the affirmative uses of whatever limitations it might experience. In these cases, the indigo-ray workings are often of aid.

The questioner, Don Elkins, sees the primary thing of importance in service-to-others path is the development of an attitude developed through meditation, ritual, and the developing appreciation for the creation or Creator, which results in a state of mind that can be expressed as an increase in vibration or oneness with all. Ra then expanded on that by suggesting that those qualities can be added to by the living day by day and moment by moment, for the true adept lives more and more as it is. (Also, without caring how others perceive them, so being more of who you are without caring what others think or say.)

Jordyn: "For raising the positive polarity charity is great, giving to others and helping others, loving and forgiving others, living in harmony with others, not infringing on their free will, not trying to have power over others and not trying to control anyone. For everyone learns at a different pace and all will end up at the same destination when we all merge back into the Creator at the seventh density harvest of this octave or universe.

My unique service to others is me sacrificing my time of play to write these books and do these YouTube videos as I give people the truth about everything in this life for their own enlightenment if they do so choose to accept. This has given me peace, healing, a calm spirit and more happiness in my life."

Jordyn: "What raised my vibration 10 percent in the month of May 2024 alone was signing a lease to help my brother have a place to live. I also spent more money on others to help them out, instead of only spending on myself. With a giving heart can make some people take advantage of that, so having equal give and take can be important. I also spent money that I'd usually use for crypto or stock investments and used it to edit my YouTube videos and publish these types of books to be more of a service to humanity. Thus, my money switched from investments only for myself and my family to investing on books and videos to get this information out to as many people as possible."

There is an infinite number of possible energy transfers between two or more mind/body/spirit complexes. For each mind/body/spirit complex is unique.

Ra: "This entity (Carla) still has transferred energy available, but we find rapidly increasing distortions towards pain in the neck, the dorsal area, and the wrists and manual appendages."

The physical energy transfer may be done numerous ways. We shall give two examples. Each begins with some sense of the self as Creator or in some way the magical personality being invoked. This may be consciously or unconsciously done. Firstly, that exercise of which we have spoken called the exercise of fire: this is, through physical energy transfer, not that which is deeply involved in the body complex combinations. Thusly the transfer is subtle, and each transfer unique in what is offered and what is accepted. At this point we may note that this is the cause for the infinite array of possible energy transfers.

The second energy transfer of which we would speak is the sexual energy transfer. This takes place upon a nonmagical level by all those entities which vibrate green ray active. It is possible, as in the case of this instrument which dedicates itself to the service of the One Infinite Creator, to further refine this energy transfer. When the other self also dedicates itself in service to the One Infinite Creator, the transfer is doubled. Then the amount of energy transferred is dependent only upon the amount of polarized sexual energy created and released. There are refinements from this point onward, leading to the realm of the high sexual magic.

In the realm of the mental bodies, there are variations of mental energy transferred. This is, again, dependent upon the knowledge sought and the knowledge offered. The most common mental energy transfer is that of the teacher and the pupil. The amount of energy is dependent upon the quality of this offering upon the part of the teacher and regards the purity of the desire to serve, and the quality of information offered and, upon the part of the student, the purity of the desire to learn and the quality of the mind vibratory complex which receives knowledge.

Another form of mental energy transfer is that of the listener and the speaker. When the speaker is experiencing mental/emotional complex distortions towards anguish, sorrow, or other mental pain, from what we have said before, you may perhaps garner knowledge of the variations possible in this transfer.

The spiritual energy transfers are the heart of all energy transfers as a knowledge of self and other self as Creator is paramount, and this is spiritual work. The varieties of spiritual energy transfer include those things of which we have spoken this day as we spoke upon the subject of the adept."

The instrument has no awareness of the pain or other sensations. However, Ra uses the yellow-ray activated physical body as a channel through which they speak. As the mind/body/spirit complex of the instrument leaves the physical shell in Ra's keeping, it is finely adjusted to their contact.

However, the pain that the instrument can't feel, when sufficiently severe, mitigates against proper contact and, when the increased distortion is violent, can cause the tuning of the channel to waver. This tuning must then be corrected, which Ra may do as the instrument offers Ra this opportunity.

Ra: "We may not teach/learn for any other to the extent that we become learn/teachers. Therefore, we shall make some general notations upon this interesting subject and allow the questioner to consider and further refine any queries.

Ra: "The archetypical mind may be defined as that mind peculiar to the Logos of the planet. Thusly, unlike the great cosmic all mind, it contains the material which it pleased the Logos to offer as refinements to the great cosmic beingness. The archetypical mind, then, is that which contains all facets which may affect mind or experience.

The magician was named as a significant archetype. However, it was not recognized that this portion of the archetypical mind represents not a portion of the deep subconscious but the conscious mind and more especially the will. The archetype called by some the High Priestess, then, is the corresponding intuitive or subconscious faculty.

Let us observe the entity as it is in relationship to the archetypical mind. You may consider the possibilities of utilizing the correspondences between the mind/body/spirit in microcosm and the archetypical mind/body/spirit closely approaching the Creator. For instance, in your ritual performed to purify this place, you use the term "Ve Geburah." It is a correct assumption that this is a portion or aspect of the One Infinite Creator. However, there are various correspondences with the archetypical mind which may be more and more refined by the adept. "Ve Gedulah" has correspondences to Jupiter, to femaleness, to the negative, to that portion of the Tree of Life concerned with Auriel.

We could go forward with more and more refinements of these two entries into the archetypical mind. We could discuss color correspondences, relationships with other archetypes, and so forth. This is the work of the adept, not the teach/learner. We may only suggest that there are systems of study which may address themselves to the aspects of the archetypical mind, and it is well to choose one and study carefully. It is more nearly well if the adept goes beyond whatever has been written and make such correspondences that the archetype can be called upon at will."

The indigo center is indeed most important for the work of the adept. However, it cannot, no matter how crystallized, correct to any extent whatsoever imbalances or blockages in other energy centers. They must need to be cleared seriatim (in order) from red upwards.

The indigo ray is the ray of the adept. There is an identification between the crystallization of that energy center and the improvement of the working of the mind/body/spirit as it begins to transcend space/time balancing and to enter the combined realms of space/time (incarnation) and time/space (non-physical).

The disciplined personality, when faced with another self, has all centers balanced according to its unique balance. Thusly the other self looks in a mirror seeing its self.

The disciplines of the personality are the paramount work of any who have become consciously aware of the process of evolution.

128

The heart of the discipline of the personality: 1- Know yourself. 2-Become the Creator. 3-Accept yourself.

The third step, when accomplished, renders (gives) one the most humble servant of all, transparent in personality and completely able to know and accept other selves. In relation to the pursuit of the magical working, the continuing discipline of the personality involves the adept in knowing its self, accepting its self, and thus clearing the path towards the great indigo gateway to the Creator. To become the Creator is to become all that there is. There is, then, no personality in the sense with which the adept begins its learn/teaching. As the consciousness of the indigo ray becomes more crystalline, more work may be done; more may be expressed from intelligent infinity.

A working of service to others has the potential of alerting a great mass of light strength.

There are sound vibratory complexes which act like the dialing of a phone. When they are appropriately vibrated with accompanying will and concentration, it is as though many upon our metaphysical or inner planes received a telephone call. They answer this call by the attention of your working.

If all people in your churches were adepts consciously full of will, of seeking, of concentration, of conscious knowledge of the calling, there would be no difference between them and those specifically magical incantations (words used as a magic spell) used by the adept. The efficacy(effectiveness) of the calling is a function of the magical qualities of those who call; that is, their desire to seek the altered state of consciousness desired.

The channeling group (Don, Carla and Jim) agreed upon the Banishing Ritual of the Lesser Pentagram for the protective ritual used before channeling Ra. The sound vibratory complexes (also known as words) used in this banishing ritual are the type of words used for altering those of the inner planes (calling positive entities such as guides, angels or Arc Angels for whatever reason

129

it may be for. The ritual calls the positive or service to others power available, just as when people pray to a so-called "God", they are attempting to call this so-called God and this call is going to many beings upon our metaphysical/inner planes on the positive/service-to-others path. Perhaps 5th, 6th and 7th density positive entities and/or angelic beings.

It is most important for the adept to feel its own growth as teach/learner. The efficiency of the ritual is the practitioner's ability to invoke the magical personality is of paramount importance. This is a study in itself. With the appropriate emotional will, polarity, and purity, work may be done with or without proper sound vibration complexes. However, there is no need for the blunt instrument when the scalpel is available.

The sounding of some of our Hebrew and some of our Sanskrit vowels have power before time and space and represent configurations of light which built all that there is. These sounds have this power because of the correspondence in vibratory complex is mathematical.

The users of these sounds in Hebrew, determined what these sounds were from the entity known as Yahweh. Yahweh aided this knowledge through impression upon the material of genetic coding which became language.

In the case of Sanskrit, the sound vibrations are pure due to the lack of previous alphabet or letter naming. Thus, the sound vibration complexes seemed to fall into place as from the Logos. This was a more natural or unaided situation or process.

SESSION 75: 10-31-1981

Ra seems to suggest that any "light worker" will, if successful in their work, attract some sort of negatively oriented psychic greeting. Just as the instrument in this group is getting psychic greetings/attacks that doesn't cause her physical pain.

130

Twice during the "Benedictus" portion of the music in a group concert she (Carla) sang as she experienced a psychic attack.

Ra: "In the singing, portion of hallows as the Mass, which immediately precedes that which is the chink called the "Hosanna," there is an amount of physical exertion required that is exhausting to any entity. This portion of which we speak is termed the "Sanctus." We come now to the matter of interest.

When the entity Jehoshuah (Jesus in the Bible) decided to return to the location called Jerusalem for the holy days of its people, it turned from work mixing love and wisdom and embraced martyrdom, which is the work of love without wisdom.

The "Hosanna," as it is termed, and the following "Benedictus," is that which is the written summation of what was shouted as Jehoshuah came into the place of its martyrdom. The general acceptance of this shout, "Hosanna to the son of David! Hosanna in the highest! Blessed is he who comes in the name of the Lord!," by that which is called the church has been a mis-statement, an occurrence which has been, perhaps, unfortunate for it is more distorted than much of the so-called Mass.

There were two factions present to greet Jehoshuah; firstly, a small group of those which hoped for an earthly king. However, Jehoshuah rode upon an ass (donkey) stating by its very demeanor that it was no earthly king and wished no fight with Roman or Sadducee.

The greater number were those which had been instructed by rabbi and elder to make jest of this entity, for those of the hierarchy feared this entity who seemed to be one of them, giving respect to their laws and then, in their eyes, betraying those time-honored laws and taking the people with it.

The chink for this instrument is this subtle situation which echoes down through your space/time and, more than this, the place the "Hosanna" holds as the harbinger (going before to announce another person) of that turning to martyrdom. We may speak only generally here. The instrument did not experience the full force of the greeting, which it correctly identified during the "Hosanna," due to the intense concentration necessary to vibrate its portion of that composition. However, the "Benedictus" in this particular rendition of these words is vibrated by one entity. Thus, the instrument relaxed its concentration and was immediately open to the fuller greeting."

(It appears entities are more protected in groups while meditating, singing or channeling.)

The chink is what turns to martyrdom. Jesus taking the path of martyrdom is the chink. It is aware of certain overbalances towards love, even to martyrdom, but has not yet, to any significant degree, balanced these distortions. Ra does not imply that this course of unbridled compassion has any fault, but affirm its perfection. It is an example of love which has served as beacon to many.

For those that seek further, the consequences of martyrdom must be considered, for in martyrdom lies the end of the opportunity in the density of the martyr, to offer love and light. Each entity must seek its deepest path.

The Orion entity finds a chink in any entity identifying in any amount toward martyrdom. It is then open by its free will to be a target for the Orion's to make it a martyr or to attack. Those involved in and dedicated to work which is magical or extremely polarized are then targeted by negative entities. (Just like negative entities are responsible for killing Jesus as I spoke about in the section of this book about Jesus' life and in my book *Correcting Distortions of The Bible*.)

The channeling group of Don, Carla and Jim entered this work with polarity but virtual innocence as to the magical nature of this polarity. That this group is beginning to discover.

132

(Just as there are psychic attacks during these channelings, there were also psychic attacks when the instrument sung songs at her church.)

It is extremely rare for an entity to attract the attention of an Orion light being. This is a most unique circumstance.

The instrument, Carla Reuckert, has an intense devotion to the teachings and example of Jesus. This entity then vibrates in song a most demanding version, called The Mass in B Minor by Bach, of this exemplary votive (sacrificial vow) complex of sound vibration. She is consciously identifying with each part of this Mass. Only thusly was the chink made available. It is not an ordinary occurrence and would not have happened had any ingredient been left out: exhaustion, bias in belief complexes, attention from an Orion entity, and the metaphysical nature of that particular set of words.

This fifth-density negative entity wishes to remove the instrument. This instrument is being greeted by a fifth-density entity which has lost some negative polarity due to its lack of dictatorship over the disposition of the instrument's mind/body/spirit or its yellow-ray-activated physical complex.

There are many Wanderers whom you may call adepts who do no conscious work in the present incarnation. It is a matter of attention. One may be a fine catcher of your game sphere, but if the eye is not turned as this sphere is tossed, then per (by) chance it will pass the entity by. If it turned its eyes upon the sphere, catching would be easy. In the case of wanderers which seek to recapitulate the degree of adeptness which each had acquired previous to this life experience, we may note that even after the forgetting process has been penetrated, there is still the yellow-activated body which does not respond as does the adept which is of green or blue-ray-activated body. Thusly, you may see the inevitability of frustrations and confusion due to the inherent difficulties of manipulating the finer forces of consciousness through the chemical apparatus of the yellow-ray-activated body.

133

Before surgery, it is well for each in this channeling group to realize its self as the Creator. Thusly each may support each other, including the support of self by humble love of self as Creator.

Certain Hebrew and Sanskrit sound vibratory complexes are powerful because they are mathematically related to the creation. The linkage is mathematical or of a musical ratio. There are those whose mind might try to attempt to resolve this mathematical ratio, but at present the coloration of the intoned vowel is part of the vibration, which cannot be accurately measured. However, it is equivalent to types of rotation of Earth's primary material particles.

When certain sounds are correctly vibrated, the creation sings. This is the concept of sympathetic resonance.

In some cases, only intoned vowel has a resonant nature. In other cases, most notably Sanskrit combinations, the selection of harmonic intervals is also of resonant nature. The creation becomes more and more contained within the practitioner if the adept uses this resonant quality.

Ra cannot tell the group of the musical notes to be intoned that are of this quality. As their seeking continues, there will be added to empirical data that acuity of sensibility which continue working in the ways of the adept offers.

Empirical data is the information acquired by scientists or whomever through experimentation and observation.

There is a great probability/possibility that if the group follows in the path that they tread now that more efficacious (intended result; effective) methods for the entire group will be established than the exercise of the fire.

Ra mentioned that hair is an antenna. It is difficult for Ra to expand on how it works due to the metaphysical nature of this

134

antennae effect. Our physics are concerned with measurements in our physical complex of experience. The metaphysical nature of the contact of those in time/space is such that the hair, as it has significant length, becomes a type of electrical battery which stays charged and tuned and is then able to aid contact even when there are small anomalies in the contact.

The inner limit of the length of hair for this aid is 4 to 4-and-one-half inches depending on the strength of the contact and the nature of the instrument.

Any entity may at any time instantaneously clear and balance its energy centers. Thus, in many cases those normally quite blocked, weakened, and distorted may, through love and strength of will, become healers momentarily. To be a healer by nature, one must indeed train its self in the disciplines of the personality.

When the magical personality is properly and efficaciously (effectively) invoked, the self has invoked its Higher Self. Thus, a bridge between space/time and time/space is made, and the sixth-density magical personality experiences directly the third-density catalyst for the duration of the working. It is most central to deliberately take off the magical personality after the working in order that the Higher Self resume its appropriate configuration as analog to the space/time (physical) mind/body/spirit (incarnated being). This should be fastidiously (meticulously) accomplished either in mind or by gesture as well if this is of significant aid.

Fastidious means being very attentive to and concerned about accuracy and detail.

The magical personality (a being of unity, 6th density, equivalent to Higher Self and a personality enormously rich in variety of experiences and subtlety of emotion.)

In the invocation (summoning or calling to bring forth) of the magical personality, it is not necessarily effective for the neophyte (person new to the subject). The magical personality begins to reside in the neophyte in small degrees or percentages as the neophyte becomes more adept.

Attention must be paid to each aspect of power, love and wisdom in developing the basic tool of the adept; that is, its self, in the three aspects of the magical personality. It is by no means a personality of three aspects. It is a being of unity, a being of 6th density, and equivalent to your Higher Self, and at the same time is a personality enormously rich in variety of experience and subtlety of emotion.

The three aspects are given that the neophyte not abuse the tools of its trade but rather approach those tools balanced in the center of love and wisdom and thus seeking power in order to serve.

A good sequence for the developing of the magical personality would be alternate meditations.

> 1- First on Power. 2- Then a meditation on love. 3- Then a meditation on wisdom. Then, cycling that way is an appropriate technique.

Visualization may be personalized and much love and support within the group generated. (Within this channeling group.)

The Adept: Each entity is the Creator. The entity, as it becomes more and more conscious of its self, gradually comes to the turning point at which it determines to seek either in service to others or in service to self. The seeker becomes the adept when it has balanced with minimal adequacy the energy centers red, orange, yellow, and blue with the addition of the green for the positive, thus moving into indigo work.

The adept then begins to do less preliminary or outer work, having to do with function, and begins to affect the inner work

136

having to do with being. As the adept becomes a more and more consciously crystallized entity, it gradually manifests more and more of what it has always been since before time, that is, the One Infinite Creator.

END OF BOOK #3 of 5

~~~

Keep in Touch:

STAY IN TOUCH! Add us, and let's be friends, or just follow to get free information that will rapidly change your life for the better.

~Email: authorkathrynjordyn@gmail.com

YouTube channel: http://youtube.com/@Kathryn_Jordyn

(This channel will talk about BMX, personal things, inspirational things, wisdom, thoughts, knowledge, and metaphysical concepts on spirituality and a little about crypto and making money.) (I'm putting it all on the line, so I invite you to check out my channel, I'm also going to be talking about Metaphysics, the Law of One, and the Truth about Jesus and the Bible.)

Instagram= @AuthorKathrynJordyn

TikTok= @kathrynjordyn

Facebook= Kathryn Jordyn

~ I found my soulmate and started to manifest after I put my all into serving others after making sure my own needs were met first, as we both are around 85-90% positively-oriented service-to-others, which of course fluctuates. ~

*Come along for the Ride, for future projects and videos.

Shop for Charity:

http://author-kathryn-jordyn.printify.me/

www.ingramcontent.com/pod-product-compliance
Lightning Source LLC
Chambersburg PA
CBHW031552040426
42452CB00006B/285

9 781735 043869